Encyclopedia
of Transportation

Volume 4

Macmillan Reference USA/An Imprint of The Gale Group
New York

Developed for Macmillan Library Reference USA by
    Visual Education Corporation, Princeton, NJ.

For Macmillan

Publisher: Elly Dickason

Senior Editor: Hélène G. Potter

Cover Design: Judy Kahn

For Visual Education

Project Director: Darryl Kestler

Writers: John Haley, Charles Roebuck,
    Rebecca Stefoff, Bruce Wetterau

Editors: Cindy George, Doriann Markey,
    Charles Roebuck

Associate Editor: Eleanor Hero

Copyediting Manager: Maureen Pancza

Indexer: Sallie Steele

Production Supervisor: Anita Crandall

Design: Maxson Crandall

Electronic Preparation: Cynthia C. Feldner,
    Fiona Torphy

Electronic Production: Rob Ehlers,
    Lisa Evans-Skopas, Isabelle Ulsh

Macmillan Reference USA
1633 Broadway
New York, NY 10019

PRINTED IN THE UNITED STATES OF AMERICA
1 2 3 4 5 6 7 8 9 10

Library of Congress Cataloging-in-Publication Data

Encyclopedia of transportation.
    p.   cm.
    "Editorial board: Enoch J. Durbin . . . [et al.]"--v. 1, p.   .
    Includes bibliographical references and index.
    Summary: An encyclopedia covering different methods
of transportation and key events, people, and social, economic, and political issues in the history of transportation.
    ISBN 0-02-865361-0 (6 vol. set)
    1. Transportation Encyclopedias.   [1. Transportation
Encyclopedias.] I. Durbin, Enoch.   II. Macmillan Reference USA.
HE141.E53   1999
388´.03--dc21   99-33371
                                                          CIP

Motorcycles

A motorcycle is any vehicle propelled by an engine and riding on two or three wheels. Most motorcycles are built like bicycles, with two wheels in line, a seat over the rear wheel, and handlebars for steering. Like a bicyclist, the motorcyclist sits exposed to wind and weather. Some people rely on motorcycles for transportation, while others use them for recreation and sport.

Manufacturers produce many types of motorcycles, from low-powered motor scooters designed for city streets to high-powered superbikes intended for racecourses. Most motorcycles can reach high speeds, use gasoline efficiently, and cost less than automobiles. Their engines are similar to those in automobiles but usually have fewer cylinders.

Development of the Motorcycle. The first motorcycles were bicycles with engines—similar to what is now called a moped. Edward Butler put an engine on a tricycle in 1884, and Gottlieb Daimler motorized a bicycle in 1885. Other European manufacturers experimented with motorcycle designs in the 1890s, and the first practical models soon appeared. American companies followed, including Indian in 1901 and Harley-Davidson in 1903. During World War I, some armies used motorcycles to carry messages and even weapons on the battlefield. In civilian life, the automobile quickly surpassed the motorcycle in popularity. Interest in motorcycles resurfaced after World War II. Since the 1970s Japanese manufacturers such as Honda and Yamaha have produced a majority of the world's larger motorcycles.

The drawing shows the main parts of a motorcycle.

Parts of a Motorcycle

Windshield
Mirror
Headlight
Wheel
Disk brake
Fuel tank
Engine
Seat
Footrest
Rear shock absorber (suspension)
Taillight
Exhaust pipe

Motorcycle Marathon

Motorcyclists participating in the annual Dakar Rally through Africa begin their 18-day trek in Granada, Spain. The first stage of the race takes them to the Spanish coast, where they board ferries and cross the Strait of Gibraltar to Morocco. Each day, riders compete to win another stage of the rally. Changing weather conditions, a twisting course through unfamiliar terrain, and nighttime riding are among the challenges that test the competitors' skill and endurance. The route continues through Morocco, Mauritania, Mali, and Burkina Faso to Dakar, Senegal, where an overall winner is declared.

suspension system of springs and other parts that supports the body of a vehicle on the axles

maneuver to make a series of changes in course

Modern Motorcycles. Motorcycles come in a wide range of sizes. The most popular are middleweight models that weigh around 450 pounds (200 kg) and have a top speed of about 90 miles (145 km) per hour.

Motorcycles intended for paved roads include street bikes and the larger road bikes. Windshields, luggage compartments, and other equipment are added in touring bikes, designed for long-distance travel on major roads and highways. Off-road motorcycles include minibikes and trail bikes, which can handle rough terrain, such as dirt roads and hills. Although these vehicles tend to be less powerful than road bikes and touring bikes, they have better **suspension** to lessen the impact of a bumpy ride.

Motor scooters are low-powered, compact vehicles used mostly for city driving. They are especially popular in Italy. Unlike other motorcycles, scooters have flat platforms on which the rider's feet rest.

In some communities, motorcycles are used by law enforcement officers to **maneuver** quickly and easily through streets clogged with automobiles. Because of the speed and agility of these vehicles, some people find them exciting to race. Different types of motorcycle racing tend to emphasize either speed or skill. For instance, road racing features machines called superbikes, which reach top speeds of around 185 miles (298 km) per hour. Motocross racing, which originated in Europe, places its competitors on a rough dirt course with obstacles and hills. It demands great endurance and skill from both riders and cycles. *See also* BICYCLES; DAIMLER, GOTTLIEB; MOPEDS.

Mountaineering

meteorological having to do with weather

geological having to do with the Earth

Mountaineering, the sport of climbing mountains, can be one of the most challenging forms of travel. The term is usually applied to snow and ice climbing on the slopes of high peaks, though it may also refer to hiking at low elevations.

Mountaineering as a sport is a fairly recent development. From ancient times until the mid-1700s, people ascended mountains to build altars to their gods, to survey the countryside, or to make **meteorological** or **geological** observations. In 1760 a Swiss scientist offered a prize to the first person to reach the top of Mont Blanc, the highest peak in the Alps at 15,771 feet (4,807 m). Two climbers finally met the challenge in 1786.

The exciting new sport gained appeal among outdoor enthusiasts in Europe, and by the 1870s climbers had reached the summits of all the major Alpine peaks. They then shifted their focus to finding new and more difficult routes to the tops of those peaks and to scaling the mountain ranges of Asia, Africa, and the Americas. In 1953 Sir Edmund Hillary of New Zealand and Tenzing Norgay of Nepal became the first climbers to conquer the world's tallest mountain, the 20,029-foot (6,105-m) Mt. Everest in Asia's Himalaya range.

The three phases of mountaineering are hiking, rock climbing, and snow and ice climbing. Basic mountaineering equipment includes sturdy, lace-up boots with cleats for traction, rope, and hardware such as crampons (metal spikes that attach to climbing boots to grip ice and snow), pitons (spikes that can be driven into rock or ice walls to hold safety ropes), and carabiners (snap links through which the rope is strung). Most climbers who attempt to scale peaks follow what is known as the expedition style of mountaineering. After assembling a large group and ample supplies, they set up a series of camps at progressively higher points on the mountain. Those seeking an even greater challenge may choose Alpine-style climbing. Beginning at the base, these climbers rapidly scale the mountain with only the equipment and supplies they can carry in their packs. Climbers usually descend from high elevations by rappeling, or sliding down the climbing rope.

Mountaineering is widely popular in North America, the British Isles, and the countries of south central Europe. Because the sport requires training and experience, climbers generally improve their skills and gain confidence through classes and clubs. *See also* ALTITUDE; HEALTH ISSUES; WALKING.

Moving and Storage

The rapid progress of transportation and communication since 1900 has transformed the United States into a highly mobile society. Many people move several times in their lives, and businesses relocate more often than in the past. Such a society requires efficient systems for transporting and storing goods during local and long-distance moves.

Local. Individuals and businesses planning a local move generally arrange to transport their belongings by truck. Relocating can involve a major investment of time and effort for an individual, family, or corporation, but a moving company with large trucks can handle even complex moves without difficulty. Moving companies provide trucks of various sizes, professional drivers, and a crew to pack boxes if needed, load, and unload the truck.

To save money, some people rent a truck and move their own possessions. They load the truck themselves, drive it to their new location, unload it, and return it to the rental agency. Rental costs are usually far less than the fees charged by moving companies, but customers must perform all of the heavy work themselves.

For local moves, some people rent a truck to transport their belongings. Long-distance relocations, however, may involve hiring a moving company to handle the packing and shipping.

Long-Distance. Moves involving somewhat greater distances are similar to local moves. Goods usually travel by truck, although they may take a few days to arrive. Moving companies sometimes combine loads from more than one customer in a large truck, for delivery along the way. Some movers offer intermodal service, a system involving more than one type of transportation during a journey. The customer's goods are packed into boxlike containers that can be shipped by truck or rail. The mover takes the containers by truck to a rail depot, where they are loaded onto a freight train for the next stage of the journey. When the train arrives at a station near the customer's destination, another mover unloads the containers and then delivers them by truck.

Moving overseas generally involves another variation of intermodal shipping. Goods packed in a container travel by truck to a port or airport, where the container is loaded on a ship or airplane. On arrival in the destination country, the goods are carried by truck to the customer's new home or business site.

Storage. People sometimes need to place their goods in storage at some stage during a move. For example, families who move out of their old homes before their new homes are available may temporarily leave household items in a storage **facility.** Movers sometimes provide storage space for their customers' possessions.

facilities something built or created to serve a particular function

Similarly, businesses that are in the process of moving may place their equipment and office furnishings in temporary storage. Companies that produce manufactured items, industrial materials, or agricultural products also use storage facilities and warehouses to hold goods awaiting distribution. Depending on the industry, they may use trucks, trains, ships, or even pipelines to transport their merchandise to storage centers. *See also* CONTAINERIZATION; FREIGHT; INTERMODAL TRANSPORT; TRADE AND COMMERCE; TRUCKING INDUSTRY; TRUCKS.

Nader, Ralph
American activist

Leader of the consumer protection movement, Ralph Nader published his book Unsafe at Any Speed in 1965.

Lawyer Ralph Nader launched the product safety and consumer protection movements in the United States in the 1960s. His activities brought major changes in the automobile industry.

Born in 1934 in Winsted, Connecticut, Nader graduated from Princeton University and Harvard Law School. Early in his legal career, he became concerned about the high number of auto accidents and related deaths. Research convinced him that the American automobile industry focused on making faster cars and increasing profits while spending little money on research to improve passenger safety.

In 1965 Nader published *Unsafe at Any Speed,* a book that criticized the American auto industry and called for reform. Nader singled out the General Motors Corporation and its Corvair automobile for attack. Despite protests from the auto industry, Nader's accusations attracted the attention of the public and the government. As a result of his work, the U.S. Congress passed the 1966 National Traffic and Motor Vehicle Safety Act, which allowed the government to set safety regulations for all cars sold in the United States. By the late 1980s, automakers began making air bags standard equipment, a safety measure that Nader had recommended for more than a decade.

Nader has looked at many aspects of American life with a critical eye. He and other investigators inspired by his work have studied and reported on food additives, coal mine safety and health, high automobile insurance costs, and other consumer protection issues. *See also* AUTOMOBILE INDUSTRY; AUTOMOBILES.

NASA

facilities *something built or created to serve a particular function*

probe *uncrewed spacecraft sent out to explore and collect information in space*

Soviet Union *nation that existed from 1922 to 1991, made up of Russia and 14 other republics in eastern Europe and northern Asia*

cosmonaut *Russian term for a person who travels into space; literally, "traveler to the universe"*

lunar *referring to the Moon*

The National Aeronautics and Space Administration (NASA) is an independent agency within the U.S. federal government that is responsible for space research and exploration. NASA **facilities** have built and sent into orbit hundreds of artificial satellites. Its deep space **probes** have fanned out across the solar system, traveling to every planet except Pluto. The crewed space flight programs—especially the visits of astronauts to the Moon in the late 1960s and early 1970s—rank among NASA's greatest accomplishments.

Early Missions.   NASA was formed in response to the emerging "space race" of the late 1950s. During the Cold War of the time, the United States and the **Soviet Union** competed aggressively for power and prestige in the world. Technology—and space missions in particular—became a major focus of this rivalry. When the Soviets launched *Sputnik 1*, the world's first artificial satellite, in October 1957, many Americans worried that the United States was falling behind in the space race. Defense officials also feared that Soviet rockets might someday carry atomic weapons toward the United States.

Responding to these concerns, President Dwight Eisenhower decided to create a civilian agency to unify American efforts at space exploration. With the approval of Congress, the existing National Advisory Committee for Aeronautics (NACA) was reorganized as NASA in mid-1958, and various space-related projects run by the military were transferred to the new agency.

The first successful U.S. venture into space had occurred earlier that year. Launched by the army on January 31, 1958, the *Explorer 1* satellite soared 1,529 miles (2,460 km) above the Earth, higher than the Soviet Sputniks. At that height, the *Explorer* discovered areas of intense radiation surrounding the Earth, later called the Van Allen radiation belts. Hundreds of NASA satellites and space probes eventually followed, including the Vanguard, Mariner, Pioneer, Viking, and Voyager series. However, crewed space flights remained the top priority for the 1960s.

Race to the Moon.   Like the satellite launches, NASA's efforts to put astronauts in orbit began as a feverish attempt to catch up with the Soviets. The Soviet **cosmonaut** Yuri Gagarin orbited the Earth in April 1961. The Americans did not duplicate this feat until February 1962, when John Glenn orbited the Earth three times in a cramped metal capsule called *Friendship 7*. By that time, President John F. Kennedy had already committed the United States to an even more ambitious goal—landing an astronaut on the Moon before the end of the decade.

NASA's budget swelled as it raced to beat the Soviets to this goal. The Apollo **lunar** landing program suffered a tragic setback in January 1967, when three of its astronauts died in a fire on the launchpad. But flights resumed, and a series of Apollo missions tested the Apollo spacecraft in Earth and lunar orbit. On July 20, 1969, *Apollo 11* landed on the lunar surface, followed by five more landings in the next three years.

Changing Direction.   The euphoria of Apollo's success soon faded. The landings had cost billions of dollars, and the nation faced urgent problems at home and abroad that demanded its attention and

The photo shows a launching of the space shuttle Discovery on September 9, 1994, from NASA's center at Cape Canaveral, Florida. NASA is the federal agency responsible for space research and exploration.

resources. NASA underwent a painful transition to smaller budgets and limited goals. The agency laid off about 10,000 employees and shelved ambitious projects like landing astronauts on Mars.

Among NASA's achievements in the 1970s were three missions to the *Skylab* space station, which housed crews of astronauts and provided valuable scientific information and experience. In 1976 two Viking probes searched for life on Mars. The following year two Voyager probes explored the outer planets.

In 1981 a new crewed vehicle, the space shuttle, began regular orbital flights. Despite the disastrous explosion of the shuttle *Challenger* in 1986, space flight came to seem fairly routine. The urgency that drove NASA's early missions had disappeared by the time the Cold War ended in the late 1980s and the Soviet Union disbanded in 1991.

Modern Missions.   U.S. political leaders realized that keeping the lead in space exploration was no longer vital to the nation's security. In the 1990s NASA modified its goals to focus on small-scale, unpiloted flights that would require less time and money than the grand missions of the past. Some of the agency's triumphs include the orbiting Hubble Space Telescope, which conducted astronomical observations above the Earth's atmosphere; the *Galileo* probe to the planet Jupiter; and the Mars Pathfinder mission that landed a robotic space vehicle on the martian surface.

The major exception to this strategy is NASA's participation, with several other national and multinational space agencies, in the construction of the International Space Station (ISS). The station is intended to serve as a platform for scientific study and to provide valuable information about the effects of long-term stays in space. It may also act as a stepping stone to what some scientists and politicians consider the next big challenge for NASA—landing astronauts on Mars.

Organization and Facilities. At the end of the twentieth century, NASA employed about 21,000 scientists and operated about a dozen facilities for conducting research and launching spacecraft. Its headquarters is located in Washington, D.C. For administrative purposes, NASA is divided into four program offices. The Office of Space Flight oversees piloted and unpiloted missions, including the space shuttle. The Office of Aeronautics, Exploration, and Technology develops equipment for space exploration. The Office of Space Science is responsible for scientific research on space and the solar system. The Office of Tracking and Data Acquisition operates three worldwide networks that monitor spacecraft and receive the information they transmit.

The Kennedy Space Center at Cape Canaveral, Florida, is NASA's major launch center. The Johnson Space Center in Houston, Texas, develops and manages piloted spacecraft. The Jet Propulsion Laboratory in Pasadena, California, handles unpiloted lunar and planetary exploration programs and operates the Deep Space Network that communicates with space probes. NASA maintains other facilities around the country, including the Marshall Space Flight Center in Huntsville, Alabama, and the Goddard Space Flight Center in Greenbelt, Maryland. NASA also works in cooperation with university laboratories and private manufacturers of spacecraft. *See also* APOLLO PROGRAM; ASTRONAUTS; CHALLENGER DISASTER; SATELLITES; SPACE EXPLORATION; SPACE ROVERS; SPACE SHUTTLES; SPACE STATIONS; SPACE TRAVEL; SPUTNIK 1.

The Space Race —Round One

The Soviets surprised and embarrassed the American government by launching *Sputnik 1,* the world's first artificial satellite, on October 4, 1957. Then a Vanguard rocket with a scientific satellite—the U.S. response to Soviet achievements in space—exploded on the launchpad.

Humiliated, officials of the American space program turned to Werner von Braun, a former German rocket engineer working for the U.S. Army. Von Braun's team hastily adapted a Jupiter-C rocket to launch *Explorer 1,* the first American satellite, on January 31, 1958.

National Road

The National Road, also called the Cumberland Road, was the first road built by the U.S. government. Originally approved by Congress in 1806, the road was intended as a way to open up the Ohio River Valley and to provide easy transport for goods to eastern markets. Although it took many years to complete, the National Road eventually extended 591 miles (951 km), from Cumberland in western Maryland to Vandalia, Illinois. Along the way it passed through parts of Pennsylvania, what is now West Virginia, Ohio, and Indiana. A smaller road extended the route to Baltimore.

Construction of the road began in 1811 and mostly followed older roads and trails. By 1818 the section from Cumberland to Wheeling,

Virginia (now in West Virginia), was complete. The federal government finished new parts of the road as far west as Columbus, Ohio, by 1833 and began working on sections leading to Vandalia. However, during the 1830s Congress turned over responsibility for the National Road to the states. Completion of the final part of the road to Vandalia, and a westward connection to St. Louis, fell to Indiana and Illinois.

A major engineering feat in its day, the National Road was 20 feet (6 m) wide with a crushed stone and gravel surface. Workers cleared a swath 66 feet (20 m) wide through forests, built bridges over rivers, and dug drainage ditches on both sides of the roadbed.

Even before the western sections were completed, the National Road proved a success. Stagecoaches and Conestoga wagons traveled between the cities and towns along the route. Delivery of goods between Pittsburgh and Baltimore took only two weeks, instead of the six to eight weeks required before the road opened.

Beginning in the 1840s, however, the road began to suffer from competition and to play a less important role in travel and trade between eastern communities and the nation's interior. It lost some traffic to the Erie Canal, completed in 1825, which provided an alternate route by water. Later, the Baltimore and Ohio Railroad was built along nearly the same route as the National Road. After the federal highway program was established in the 1920s, the National Road became U.S. Highway 40. It later joined the Interstate Highway System as Interstate 70. *See also* BALTIMORE AND OHIO RAILROAD; CONESTOGA WAGONS; ERIE CANAL; ROADS; STAGECOACHES.

National Transportation Safety Board

The National Transportation Safety Board (NTSB), an independent agency of the U.S. government, is responsible for investigating all civil aviation accidents in the United States and major collisions involving other forms of transportation. Created in 1967, the NTSB took over the duties of the Civil Aeronautics Board (CAB). At first the NTSB depended on the U.S. Department of Transportation (DOT) for funding and assistance with daily operations. However, in 1975, the government separated the two organizations.

In addition to investigating domestic air accidents, the NTSB provides personnel to look into overseas incidents involving aircraft and aircraft systems registered or manufactured in the United States. Since it began operations in 1967, the NTSB has conducted inquiries into more than 100,000 aviation accidents all over the world.

The NTSB also studies transportation problems of national significance, such as school bus safety, driving under the influence of alcohol, and truck collisions, and issues reports and offers suggestions for improvement. Although the NTSB does not have authority to enforce its proposals, more than 80 percent of its safety recommendations have been adopted. For example, a 1985 NTSB study resulted in many of the laws regulating child safety seats. Many of the safety features now found on airplanes, automobiles, trains, pipelines, and marine vessels originated with the NTSB. *See also* ACCIDENTS; CIVIL AERONAUTICS BOARD; FAA (FEDERAL AVIATION ADMINISTRATION); GOVERNMENT AND TRANSPORTATION; TRANSPORTATION, U.S. DEPARTMENT OF.

facilities something built or created to serve a particular function

A navy is a branch of the armed forces that is organized primarily to defend a nation at sea. Navies originally included all the ships in a nation—its merchant and fishing vessels as well as its warships. Over time, however, navies became specialized, professional armed forces consisting of various types of combat ships as well as the personnel, equipment, and **facilities** that support them.

Many countries have navies to protect their national interests. The forces range from small navies with a few ships for patrolling coastal operations to navies that consist of many types of ships and also have an air force. The United States has the largest and most powerful navy in the world, with hundreds of ships and planes and millions of personnel. In addition to its naval and air forces, the U.S. Navy has its own combat ground force, the U.S. Marines.

History of Navies

Few countries in ancient times had professional navies. Most ships were privately owned, and crews carried weapons to protect themselves from pirates or to attack other ships. The first national navies were assembled mainly to guard seacoasts and trade routes and to defend the country against invaders. The idea of a naval force dedicated solely to warfare did not gain much ground until after A.D. 1500.

Early Navies.   Among the earliest navies were those of the ancient Mediterranean world. In 483 B.C. the Greek city-state of Athens built a fleet to protect itself from attacks by the Persians. The Athenians became the leading naval power in the Mediterranean. Later, after defeating the Egyptian fleet at the Battle of Actium in 31 B.C., the Romans emerged as the region's great naval power. For the next 400 years Roman ships dominated the Mediterranean Sea.

After the fall of Rome in A.D. 476, no major navy arose in Europe for some time. From about 700 to the late 1000s, Norsemen from Scandinavia raided the coasts of western Europe and even sailed across the Atlantic Ocean. Several European countries, including England, built navies to defend themselves against these fierce Viking raiders.

By the 1100s European navies were being used for more than defense. They patrolled coastal waters against piracy, worked to expand and defend seaborne trade, and participated in wars of conquest. The leading naval powers in the Mediterranean during the late Middle Ages were the Italian city of Venice and the Ottoman Empire that dominated much of eastern Europe.

Rise of Modern Navies.   As European nations began building colonial empires in the late 1400s, **maritime** trade expanded. England and Spain formed navies to defend their overseas colonies and trade routes. The struggle for supremacy between these nations led to the birth of modern navies devoted largely to warfare.

Between the 1500s and 1700s, European navies grew larger and more powerful as nations competed for control of the seas. Spain dominated until 1588, when its **armada** was defeated by the English. England and

Less Is More

For many years warships grew in size with the development of bigger guns and more powerful engines. In 1900 the largest battleships weighed about 20,000 tons. By 1940 these ships were dwarfed in size by huge, 45,000-ton battleships. Recent advances in missile technology enable small ships to carry more firepower and deliver it over greater distances than large ships with conventional guns. Furthermore, giant battleships and aircraft carriers are very expensive to build, and they make easy targets. As a result, navies now tend to favor smaller vessels and submarines, which are more versatile and harder to hit.

maritime related to the sea or shipping

armada fleet of warships

the Netherlands competed for naval supremacy in the 1600s, and in the 1700s France became England's chief rival. The British victory over France at the Battle of Trafalgar in 1805 made Great Britain the world's leading naval power, a position it held for the next 100 years.

Advances in technology played an important role in the rise of modern navies. In the Middle Ages, naval vessels used machines called catapults to hurl rocks and other objects at enemy ships. By the 1500s cannons had become the most important naval weapons. Naval strategy changed as well. Before 1500, naval combat involved shooting arrows, hurling objects from catapults, and ramming and boarding enemy vessels. With the introduction of cannons, gun battles emerged as the main form of naval combat.

Technological advances in the 1800s—including the development of steam power and iron-hulled warships—revolutionized navies and naval warfare. Ships became bigger and faster, and heavy armor protected them from powerful cannons and guns. The old sailing warship had been transformed into the modern battleship.

The Twentieth Century.

The pace of change increased in the 1900s, as navies continued to grow in size and strength. Among the most significant technological advances were the development of submarines, aircraft carriers, nuclear power, and **guided missiles.**

Germany pioneered the use of submarines in World War I. Capable of traveling secretly underwater, submarines proved to be very effective weapons. In World War II the United States and Japan organized their naval fleets around aircraft carriers. The carriers allowed navies to launch air attacks on the enemy far from ground-based forces.

In 1954 the United States launched the first nuclear-powered ship, the submarine *Nautilus.* Nuclear-powered submarines can stay underwater indefinitely, a great advantage in naval operations. The development of submarine-launched missiles has made submarines even more important. Armed with nuclear warheads, these missiles can be launched against distant enemy targets while the ship is submerged. The use of nuclear-powered submarines and missiles has reduced the need for conventional battleships and aircraft carriers, thus changing the composition of modern navies.

guided missile *missile, or rocket, steered by radio signals and electronic codes*

Originally established by the Continental Congress in 1775, the U.S. Navy has grown into the most powerful naval force in the world. Its combat ships include giant aircraft carriers, such as the USS Kitty Hawk.

The United States Navy

Originally established by the Continental Congress in 1775, the U.S. Navy has grown into the most powerful naval force in the world. Responsible for defending the nation at sea, it also provides support to the other armed services of the United States.

Structure of the Navy.

The Department of the Navy is a branch of the Department of Defense. It is divided into three parts: the Navy Department, the Operating Forces, and the Shore Establishment. The Navy Department sets naval policies and supervises all operations of the U.S. Navy and the U.S. Marine Corps. The Operating Forces, which consists of the various fleets and sea commands, carries out naval policies. The Shore Establishment operates naval bases and facilities such as training centers and supply depots that support the Operating Forces.

Types of Ships. The U.S. Navy has two main categories of ships: combat ships and auxiliary ships. Combat ships include aircraft carriers, battleships, cruisers, destroyers, and submarines. The navy also has **amphibious** assault ships, used to land troops ashore, and command ships, which carry communications equipment and serve as command centers. Various types of auxiliary ships support combat ships by providing them with supplies and services. These include transport ships, which deliver fuel, ammunition, food, and spare parts to vessels at sea; maintenance and repair ships; experimental ships for testing new designs and weapons; and research and survey ships, which study and map the oceans and coastlines.

Naval Officers. The U.S. Navy includes various levels of naval officers and enlisted sailors. Naval officers are trained at the U.S. Naval Academy in Annapolis, Maryland, or at one of several officer-training programs. Some programs are specifically designed for college students, college graduates, or others not already in the navy. Others appoint officers from the lower ranks of enlisted personnel.

Depending on rank and training, naval officers perform a variety of roles, ranging from commanding ships, flying naval aircraft, or managing shore activities to performing technical or administrative tasks. Some naval officers serve as lawyers, doctors, nurses, or engineers or have other specialized roles. Many officers and enlisted men and women joined the U.S. Navy for the opportunity to learn useful skills while serving their country. *See also* AIRCRAFT, MILITARY; AIRCRAFT CARRIER; COAST GUARD; FRIGATES; GUIDED MISSILES; SHIPS AND BOATS; SHIPS AND BOATS, TYPES OF; SPANISH ARMADA; SUBMARINES AND SUBMERSIBLES; VIKINGS.

The U.S. Navy trains men and women at the U.S. Naval Academy in Annapolis, Maryland, and at other training centers around the country.

amphibious *able to move on land and through water*

Navigation

Navigation is the process of plotting a route from one point to another. A navigator must figure out where a vehicle is located at any given moment and what path it must follow to reach its desired destination. Modern navigators use a variety of methods and instruments to determine the position of vehicles at sea, in the air, in space, and on land. Some of these systems and tools are streamlined versions of ancient techniques and devices. Others, such as radar, computers, and satellites, employ modern technology.

Early History

For centuries navigation was chiefly concerned with the movement of watercraft. The word comes from the Latin *navis,* which means "ship," and *agere,* which means "to drive." When advances in technology produced

Beginning in the 1400s, navigators used the astrolabe to determine latitude by measuring the angle of the North Star or the Sun above the horizon.

meteorological *having to do with weather*

astronomical *having to do with the study of the stars, planets and so on*

latitude *distance north or south of the equator*

astrolabe *navigational instrument used since ancient times to determine distance north or south of the equator*

chronometer *clock designed to keep precise time in the rough conditions of sea travel*

longitude *distance east or west of the prime meridian, an imaginary line on the Earth's surface that runs through Greenwich, England*

aeronautical *relating to the science of flight*

new vehicles and new forms of transportation, the goals and tools of navigation also changed.

Early navigation relied on signs of nature. Mariners usually stayed within sight of land so that they could guide their ships by following familiar landmarks such as mountains and rivers. When people began making longer voyages on open waters, they used information gathered from observing the weather and the skies.

Meteorological navigation was based on the direction from which winds blow. Recognizing a familiar wind, a sailor knew its direction. Medieval sea charts called portolans had networks of lines that indicated the directions of the winds.

The magnetic compass appeared in China by A.D. 1100 and in Europe and the Near East about 100 years later. Mariners used this instrument, which is controlled by the Earth's magnetic field and is unaffected by the weather, to tell direction. Experienced sailors also gained clues to their location from tides, currents, floating vegetation, and seabird flight paths.

Astronomical navigation depended on the position of the Sun, Moon, and stars and their movements across the sky. Adopting techniques developed by early sky watchers on land, seafarers learned to determine their **latitude** by measuring the angle of the North Star or the Sun above the horizon. Beginning in the 1400s and 1500s, they borrowed tools from astronomy, the **astrolabe** and a cross-shaped wooden device called a cross-staff, to calculate the angle with greater accuracy. Later tools that served a similar purpose included the quadrant, the sextant, and the octant. Not until the mid-1700s and the invention of the **chronometer,** however, could mariners measure **longitude** at sea with any precision.

Instruments and Methods

Navigational instruments range from a simple pole used to measure water depth to artificial satellites orbiting the Earth that send out signals. Methods of navigating also vary greatly in complexity.

Equipment. The most basic navigational tool is a map or chart that represents all or part of the Earth's surface. Modern maps exist in many forms, including CD-ROMs and other computerized databases. Airplane pilots rely on **aeronautical** charts, which indicate the location of various landmarks, airline routes, landing fields, and radio stations sending air navigation signals.

The introduction of radio time signals on ships and aircraft in the early 1900s marked the beginning of electronic navigation. At about the same time, the gyroscope—a spinning wheel or sphere that resists changes in its position even when tilted—was being incorporated into navigational instruments.

Modern ships, airplanes, missiles, and spacecraft are equipped with gyroscopic devices such as accelerometers and gyrocompasses. Accelerometers measure acceleration and detect and measure vibration. An advanced version of the magnetic compass, a gyrocompass contains

sonar short for sound navigation and ranging; system that uses sound waves to locate underwater objects

a gyroscope that stays pointed toward true geographic north. These tools provide information on speed and direction of travel, making it possible for vehicles to fix their position at any time. Radar and **sonar** devices allow navigators to detect solid objects. Artificial satellites that orbit the Earth broadcast radio signals that guide craft with pinpoint precision.

Techniques. Depending on the tools available and the conditions of travel, more than one method of navigation may be employed. Piloting uses landmarks such as mountains, islands, and lighthouses to determine location. Coastal navigators have practiced piloting for thousands of years, and ships traveling close to land or in harbors still follow this method. In the days before jet travel and electronic controls, aircraft pilots also relied on piloting.

Mariners sailing away from the coast often used dead reckoning, another ancient form of navigation. The technique involves keeping track of the ship's speed and direction of travel for a period of time, then using the vessel's last-known position to estimate its new position. Because dead reckoning does not take into account possible sideways drift caused by winds or current, it is not always accurate. Some modern navigators rely on computer-aided dead reckoning combined with other methods. Giant ships, such as tankers, use the **Doppler effect** to calculate their positions.

Doppler effect change in the frequency of a wave such as light or sound as the source of the wave nears or moves away from an observer.

Astronomical navigation has not changed significantly from the days of the early mariners. Using information published in navigational almanacs and tables, modern navigators compare a heavenly body's height above the horizon with its known position when observed from certain locations on the Earth's surface. With this data the navigator can determine the vehicle's position relative to those specific locations.

Electronic navigation requires instruments that use radio signals. Such signals provide precise time checks and allow navigators to calculate their position. Loran (long-range navigation), omega, and omnirange are position-finding systems that pick up radio signals sent from fixed transmitters. Radar and sonar use electronic devices that broadcast signals. These signals bounce off objects and, when received by the sender, show what lies ahead or below.

Cars That Navigate for You

In the 1990s automobile manufacturers began producing cars with onboard navigation computers that can determine a car's position and explain how to reach a destination. The computers use the Global Positioning System (GPS) to track a car's location, and they search a database of maps to provide directions. Dashboard monitors in the car display the maps, while a computer-generated voice guides the driver. Built-in navigation systems function best in cities where the driver has a specific address for the destination.

Since the 1960s the use of artificial satellites has dramatically changed the way submarines, ships, aircraft, and even drivers and hikers navigate. As satellites circle the Earth, they broadcast radio signals at specific frequencies. Radio receivers capture the incoming radio waves and relay the information to a computer. These signals enable the computer to fix the distance between the craft and the satellite and calculate the latitude and longitude of the craft. The U.S. Naval Navigation Satellite System (NNSS) and the Global Positioning System (GPS) both have satellites. Traveling in very high orbits above the Earth's surface, GPS satellites provide extremely accurate messages regarding position and speed—day or night.

Another method of navigation known as inertial guidance is a variation of dead reckoning. It uses data gathered by gyroscopes and accelerometers to determine a vehicle's position and course. Submarines, ships, aircraft, spacecraft, and guided missiles rely on inertial guidance systems.

This sailor is using an instrument known as a sextant and a chart to calculate the position of his ship at sea.

Modern Problems

The challenges faced by early mariners were quite different from those encountered by the navigators of the modern world. Although the sailors of ancient and medieval times may have ventured into uncharted waters, they were only expected to reach their destinations, perhaps record their journeys in written reports, on maps, or on sea charts, and return home safely. In many cases, these mariners were all alone on a voyage. Modern navigators, however, must work within a crowded worldwide transportation network, and they have additional responsibilities.

At Sea. In busy ports, ships must follow rules for passing and granting right-of-way and display color-coded running lights so that other craft can easily see their position and direction. In the past, sailors had a problem with visibility at night and in fog and other bad weather. Now navigators use radar and sonar to "see" electronic images of the objects within their path at all times.

Submarines have their own set of navigational problems. Piloting and celestial navigation are impossible when these craft are fully submerged, and not all radio signals travel well through seawater. Submarine navigators rely on dead reckoning and inertial guidance systems.

Air and Space. As air travel has increased, the problem of avoiding collisions among aircraft has become a major issue. Airplane pilots receive guidance from radio beacons and air traffic controllers. Navigators of the sky must also deal with changing weather conditions, such as wind, clouds, ice, and precipitation, that can affect tight flight schedules.

Space travel presents unique navigational challenges. A spacecraft must not only follow a precise course but in many cases must also arrive at a specific time in order to complete a mission such as a space-station docking or landing. In addition, the majority of spacecraft do not have human navigators to make on-the-spot calculations and adjustments. Instead, they operate by inertial guidance systems and navigational computers that respond to instructions from control centers on Earth.

See also AIR TRAFFIC CONTROL; ASTRONOMY; COMPASS; EXPLORATION; GLOBAL POSITIONING SYSTEM (GPS); GYROSCOPE; LATITUDE AND LONGITUDE; LORAN; MAPS AND CHARTS; RADAR; SONAR.

Noise Control

decibel *unit for expressing the relative intensity of sounds*

Jet aircraft cause severe noise pollution, which affects many people who live near airports. Here, a jet flies over houses near London's Heathrow Airport.

Noise control involves the efforts of industry and government to limit the noise in modern society. Medical authorities generally agree that loud noises—those over about 90 **decibels** (db)—can have a harmful effect on human health. Excessive noise has been linked not only to damaged hearing, but also to other health problems, including reduced blood circulation, increased cholesterol, and psychological stress—all of which can contribute to high blood pressure and heart disease.

Many forms of transportation contribute to noise pollution, producing sounds that equal or exceed 90 db. The noise comes both from powerful engines and other mechanical devices and from the speed itself. A typical subway in the United States and the outboard motor of a speedboat each register about 100 db; some motorcycles can reach 110 db; and a jet plane at takeoff produces about 150 db.

Many laws and regulations have been passed to limit the noise pollution caused by transportation. All motor vehicles must have mufflers to

reduce engine noise. In the United States, cars and large motorcycles must operate at no higher than 88 db, while large trucks may produce a few decibels more. Some highways are lined with vertical walls to screen nearby neighborhoods from traffic noise.

Jet aircraft cause some of the worst noise pollution and affect a large number of people because most major airports are located in heavily populated urban areas. In some places government officials have directed airlines to plot their flight routes over less densely settled areas. However, such routes may require extra time and fuel, resulting in higher costs for airlines and passengers. Certain airports have imposed a ban on takeoffs and landings after a certain hour at night to avoid disturbing nearby residents.

The best way to reduce aircraft noise is to build quieter jet engines. Improved technology has led to the development of lower-decibel jet engines, and newer aircraft are considerably less noisy than older jets. In addition, installing "hush kits" on older engines makes them quieter. Legislation passed by the U.S. Congress in 1990 required airlines to eliminate the noisiest airplanes in service in stages over a ten-year period.

Supersonic aircraft present a slightly different problem. Their high speed breaks the **sound barrier,** producing a "sonic boom" that can be heard 30 miles (48 km) away. As a result, many nations refuse to allow supersonic planes to fly over their territory. *See also* AUTOMOBILES, EFFECTS OF; POLLUTION AND TRANSPORTATION; SUPERSONIC FLIGHT.

supersonic *faster than the speed of sound*

sound barrier *sudden increase in air resistance that occurs when an aircraft approaches the speed of sound*

Northeast Passage

The Northeast Passage is the sea route that links the Atlantic and Pacific Oceans through the Arctic waters north of Europe and Asia. For more than 300 years, ice-clogged seas prevented explorers from navigating the waterway. Today specially equipped ships called icebreakers keep the passage open in the summer months.

As early as the 900s, Norse seafarers—also known as Vikings—probed the waters north of Europe. By the 1300s the people of western Russia had established a northern sea route to Norway. With the growth of trade to distant markets in the 1500s, Europeans sought a better way to reach China and Southeast Asia. However, Portugal dominated the southern route around Africa, forcing northern and eastern neighbors to find another course to the Pacific Ocean. Between the mid-1500s and the mid-1800s, a number of European expeditions, including those of Sebastian Cabot and Henry Hudson, set off in search of a Northeast Passage. However, none reached even the halfway point.

Russian explorers, fur traders, and adventurers had more luck, by both land and sea. By the mid-1700s Russians had mapped most of their country's northern coast. Nevertheless, the ships and **maritime** technology of the time could not conquer the barrier of polar ice. Not until the late 1870s did a Swedish expedition led by Nils Nordenskiöld, aboard the steamship *Vega,* navigate the complete passage from west to east. His success launched a flurry of scientific and mapping expeditions into the Northeast Passage and the Arctic Ocean north of Russia. Trading voyages along the coast also grew more frequent, and during the 1920s the Russian government focused on the northern sea route's usefulness

maritime *related to the sea or shipping*

as a working waterway in the economic development of northern Siberia. Although heavy winter ice makes the sea route usable only four months a year, Russian naval, cargo, and scientific research ships now take the Northeast Passage during the summer. *See also* EXPLORATION; ICEBREAKERS; NORTHWEST PASSAGE; VIKINGS.

Northwest Passage

For well over 300 years, European explorers sought a northern sea route linking the Atlantic and Pacific Oceans. Driven by the promise of riches in Asia and the belief that a water passage existed, numerous expeditions tried to sail through the ice-choked waters of the Arctic islands north of Canada. Unfortunately, the majority of these attempts to find a Northwest Passage failed, some tragically.

The Search. For hundreds of years, silks, spices, and jewels from Asia traveled to European markets by overland routes through the lands bordering the Mediterranean Sea. These slow, costly journeys frustrated European princes and merchants and caused them to seek a more direct path to Asia. In the late 1400s they turned their attention to the recently discovered continent of North America. During the following centuries, much of the exploration of North America was aimed at finding a water route to Asia through or around it.

In 1497 Italian explorer John Cabot led the first English expedition to North America. Some historians believe that he landed on what is now called Newfoundland. The French sponsored Italian navigator Giovanni da Verrazano's voyage in search of a northern sea route in 1524. Although Verrazano explored a large portion of North America's coast, his attempt to find a passage through the continent was unsuccessful. Several years later French explorer Jacques Cartier probed Canada's St. Lawrence River region, but rapids put an end to his westward journey on the river.

navigable deep or wide enough for boats or ships to pass through

The English continued the search for a **navigable** route to Asia in the 1570s, when Martin Frobisher led three voyages to the waters west of Greenland. He investigated the southern coast of what became known as Baffin Island but abandoned further exploration of the region after finding what turned out to be fool's gold. About ten years later, John Davis discovered a wide waterway leading north between Greenland and Baffin Island. Although ice prevented Davis from sailing farther north, the waterway that is now called Davis Strait became a key link to the Northwest Passage.

Some of the early efforts to find a northern sea route ended in disaster. On a voyage in 1610/1611, Henry Hudson became the first person to enter Canada's Hudson Bay, but his crew members revolted after barely surviving a long, hard winter. They set Hudson and several others adrift aboard a small, open boat in the harsh Arctic waters, where the explorer and his companions died.

From 1631 to 1632, Luke Fox and Thomas James searched the western shores of Hudson Bay for an open passage. When their expeditions proved that the bay had no such outlet, explorers shifted their focus to the continent's interior. Indian stories of rivers and inland seas leading to the west inspired journeys to the Great Lakes and Mississippi River regions. But these efforts and others on the Pacific coast of North America were not successful.

The Race Resumes. By about 1800 geographers had concluded that there was no ice-free water route by which merchants could easily carry cargo between the Atlantic and Pacific Oceans. Nevertheless, after the British government offered a large cash prize to any citizen who could locate such a route, a new wave of searches for the Northwest Passage began. A series of well-equipped expeditions pushed into the northern reaches of Davis Strait and the channels that run westward through a maze of rocky, desolate islands.

The most ambitious expedition was that of Sir John Franklin of the Royal Navy in 1845. He set out with a crew of 129 men and two ships, but the large vessels became stuck in the ice-clogged waters of northern Canada and could not escape. Over a ten-year period, the British sent out 50 separate rescue missions to search for the missing explorers. Although Franklin and his men were never found, the search teams mapped large areas of Canada's Arctic coastline. In 1850 British naval commander Robert McClure set out to look for Franklin in the western waters of the Arctic Ocean. When McClure reached the Prince of Wales Strait between Banks and Victoria Islands, he became the first European to discover the northern waterway. However, ice prevented McClure from navigating the entire passage.

The Real Northwest Passage. During a voyage from 1903 to 1906, Norwegian explorer Roald Amundsen finally sailed what became known as the Northwest Passage. Located 500 miles (805 km) north of the Arctic Circle, the water route winds through narrow channels between islands for 900 miles (1,448 km) of its 3,500-mile (5,630-km) length. Polar ice makes the relatively open waters at each end of the passage particularly dangerous. Henry Larsen of the Royal Canadian Mounted Police became the first to travel the Northwest Passage in a single season in 1944.

By 1960 several nuclear-powered submarines had crossed between the Atlantic and Pacific Oceans under the polar ice. The first commercial ship through the passage was the reinforced oil tanker *Manhattan*, which carried oil from Alaska to the East Coast in 1969. However, Arctic shipping through the Northwest Passage proved too costly and dangerous for most commercial purposes. Current **maritime** traffic in the Northwest Passage consists mostly of icebreaker vessels on research missions. *See also* EXPLORATION; ICEBREAKERS; NORTHEAST PASSAGE.

maritime *related to the sea or shipping*

Oberth, Hermann
Rocket pioneer

German scientist Hermann Oberth was a pioneer in the development of liquid fuel rockets and one of the first people to think about the possibility of sending humans into space. Born in 1894 in Nagyszeben, Hungary (now part of Romania), Oberth was educated at universities in Germany and Romania. In his 1923 pamphlet *The Rocket into Interplanetary Space,* he used mathematics to demonstrate the possibility of building rockets that could carry a crew beyond the gravitational pull of Earth.

During the 1930s Oberth designed and tested liquid fuel rockets. After becoming a German citizen in 1940, he worked at Germany's rocket development center and helped design the advanced V-2 rocket used during World War II. In 1955 he moved to the United States, where he served as an adviser to the U.S. Army's missile program. Retiring to Germany in 1958, Oberth spent his later years writing and lecturing. He died in 1989. *See also* Rockets; Space Travel.

Ocean Liners

transatlantic relating to crossing the Atlantic Ocean

An ocean liner is a ship that carries passengers across the ocean on a regular schedule between certain ports. Until the expansion of commercial air travel in the 1950s, ocean liners dominated passenger transportation across the Atlantic Ocean. In some years more than a million passengers crossed the ocean by ship.

The first passenger ships to make regularly scheduled **transatlantic** crossings were American "sailing packets," which traveled between New York and England in the early 1800s carrying cargo as well as passengers. Some of these ships featured small staterooms and even dining rooms—incredible luxuries at the time.

After only a few decades, the sailing packets were replaced by steamships, and Britain began to lead the way in transatlantic travel. In 1840 Samuel Cunard, a Nova Scotian, launched a steamship service between Liverpool, England, and Boston that lasted for 125 years. Cunard ships were famous for their speed and safety.

A number of Americans tried to establish transatlantic service to compete with the Cunard Line. The most prominent was Cornelius Vanderbilt, who started a scheduled route between New York and Le Havre, France. Vanderbilt's shipping venture was cut short by the Civil War in the United States and by his growing interest in railroads.

In the mid-1800s two inventions—the screw propeller and the steam turbine—revolutionized transatlantic travel. Ships became faster, and shipbuilders now emphasized speed and comfort. Ship designers moved

Until the expansion of air travel in the 1950s, ocean liners dominated passenger transportation across the Atlantic Ocean. At the end of the twentieth century, the Queen Elizabeth 2 was the only ocean liner still making transatlantic voyages.

the best staterooms toward the middle of ships—away from noisy propellers—and stacked cabins one on top of another on several decks.

Competition for transatlantic passenger service increased after the mid-1800s and led to the construction of ever larger, faster, and more comfortable ships. Accommodations onboard ranged from the deluxe areas reserved for first-class passengers to the cramped and uncomfortable quarters below decks known as steerage class. Many immigrants who arrived in the United States between the late 1800s and 1920s traveled in steerage. Steamship service was not limited to the Atlantic Ocean. American ships also carried passengers to destinations in the Pacific.

For a short time at the turn of the century, German ships reigned over the Atlantic as the largest and fastest ocean liners afloat. Not to be outdone, the Cunard Line built the swift and luxurious *Lusitania* and *Mauretania.* The White Star Line of Britain responded by building the three largest, fastest, and most expensively appointed ships in the world—the *Olympic, Britannic,* and *Titanic.* Sunk by an iceberg during its maiden voyage in 1912, the *Titanic* sailed into the history books.

The age of ocean liners reached its peak in the 1930s with construction of the French ship *Normandie* and the British ships *Queen Mary* and *Queen Elizabeth.* The grandest luxury ships ever built, these giant ocean liners were each nearly 1,000 feet (305 m) long. During the next two decades, several other large and luxurious ocean liners were built, including the American *United States,* the Italian *Andrea Doria,* and the French *Ile de France.*

By the 1950s, commercial passenger airlines had seriously hurt transatlantic travel by sea. Flying was much faster and less expensive than sailing, and ocean liners could no longer compete effectively. Most large vessels were either retired or converted to cruise ships for sailing the Caribbean and Mediterranean Seas and other vacation areas. Only one ocean liner, the *Queen Elizabeth 2,* continued to make transatlantic voyages. *See also* CRUISE SHIPS; CUNARD LINE; GREAT EASTERN; LUSITANIA; PASSENGERS; SHIPS AND BOATS, TYPES OF; SHIPWRECKS; TRAVEL INDUSTRY.

The Queen Mary

Named for the wife of King George V of England and launched by her in September 1934, the *Queen Mary* was the fastest ocean liner of its day. In 1938 it set a speed record for the Atlantic Ocean crossing—a record that stood until the SS *United States* toppled it in 1952. During World War II the *Queen Mary* became a troop carrier, and—together with the *Queen Elizabeth*—transported 320,000 of the 865,000 American troops that sailed to Britain. In 1967, having completed a total of 1,001 Atlantic crossings, the *Queen Mary* sailed to Long Beach, California, where it became a floating hotel and museum.

Oceanography

see *Water Currents, Waves, and Tides.*

Oregon Trail

The Oregon Trail ran west from Independence, Missouri, for 2,000 miles (3,220 km) across North America. Unlike the Santa Fe Trail, the Oregon Trail was not principally a trade route. It was the highway along which thousands of settlers traveled during the mid-1800s in a mass migration that helped make the American West part of the United States.

Role in History. In the early 1800s, Great Britain and the United States both claimed the Oregon Country, which included the present-day states of Oregon and Washington and part of British Columbia in Canada. Britain's claim was based on the activities of British trading companies in the region. The American claim grew out of the Lewis and Clark expedition of 1804 to 1806, which had explored the territory between the Mississippi River and the Pacific Ocean for the U.S. government.

Soon after the return of Lewis and Clark, American fur traders and trappers entered the Far West. Missionaries followed. In the 1830s the route of the Oregon Trail was becoming established. A small party of settlers made the journey in 1841, drawn by reports of the fertile farmland and mild climate in Oregon's Willamette River valley.

In 1843 about 1,000 people gathered in Missouri, formed wagon trains, and headed west on the trail. Two years later about 3,000 travelers followed the long route to Oregon. The growing population of Americans in the Willamette Valley led Britain to sign an agreement in 1846 that gave the United States control of Oregon. After gold was discovered in California in the late 1840s, some travelers began branching off from the Oregon Trail to head south, but the migration into the Pacific Northwest continued for many years.

Traveling the Trail.   The Oregon Trail passed from Missouri through a corner of present-day Kansas, across Nebraska along the Platte River, through the Rocky Mountains in Wyoming, across southern Idaho along the Snake River, and west through Oregon over the Blue Mountains and along the Columbia River. It covered almost every kind of terrain the West had to offer: tall-grass prairie, rivers, high plains, mountains, and deserts. The five- or six-month journey to Oregon was not an undertaking for the weak.

The pioneers' wagons, pulled by horses or oxen, were about 4 feet (1.2 m) wide and 20 feet (6 m) long. The limited space inside was filled with valuable supplies, leaving no room for passengers. As a result, most people walked or rode on horseback for the entire distance. Often the animals grew too weak and weary to pull the wagons, and the settlers abandoned some of their furniture and other heavy possessions along the route.

The trail was also lined with graves. According to some estimates, as many as 30,000 people died on the trail from exposure, disease, and accidents. Another 100 or so travelers perished in conflicts with Native Americans between the 1840s and the late 1800s, when the Oregon Trail gave way to the railroads crossing the West. *See also* CARTS, CARRIAGES, AND WAGONS; LEWIS AND CLARK EXPEDITION; SANTA FE TRAIL.

The deep ruts cut by wagon wheels on the Oregon Trail remain visible on the High Plains prairie near Guernsey, Wyoming.

Orient Express

The Orient Express was a train that became a transportation legend, partly because it was the first to offer passenger service between western Europe and the Near East but mostly because of its dazzling luxury. From the 1880s to the 1930s, the Orient Express was "the king of trains and the train of kings."

In 1883 a Belgian businessman named Georges Nagelmackers launched a brand-new railway service. It featured deluxe trains in which people could travel in great comfort, remaining in the same car throughout a multiday journey and crossing national borders without inconvenience. At a time when passengers riding between New York and Chicago had to change cars five times and long railway journeys were notorious for discomfort, Nagelmackers's approach to train travel appealed to wealthy travelers.

By 1889 the Orient Express ran between Paris, France, and Constantinople (now Istanbul), Turkey. The train boasted an elegant dining car with a gourmet chef, beds with silk sheets, and magnificent works of art. The Orient Express was not for everyone—a single ticket cost about as much as the annual rent of a house in London.

World War I and the Depression of the 1930s took their toll, dimming the luxurious glow of the Orient Express. The last regular run on the Paris-to-Istanbul route took place in 1977, although special tours still use that route from time to time. In 1982 a new service, the Venice-Simplon-Orient-Express, began operating between London, England, and Venice, Italy, using restored railway cars. *See also* RAILROADS, HISTORY OF; RAILWAY TRAINS, PARTS OF.

Pacific Ocean

The Pacific Ocean is not just the world's largest body of water—it is also the world's largest surface feature. Covering an area of more than 63 million square miles (165 million square km), the Pacific has served as an important trade and transportation route for thousands of years.

Oceanic Features. To the north the Pacific meets the Arctic Ocean, and to the south it washes the icy shores of Antarctica. The Americas form the Pacific's eastern border, while Asia and the Indian Ocean create its western border. The deepest known place in any ocean is the Mariana Trench in the western Pacific, 36,198 feet (11,033 m) deep.

In the southern and eastern parts of this vast body of water, the trade winds and the westerlies blow steadily, providing reliable routes for mariners. However, weather conditions in the northern and western portions of the Pacific are not quite as constant. Tropical storms known as typhoons bring winds of at least 74 miles (119 km) per hour. Ships sailing in the areas to the east of the Philippine Islands and in the South and China Seas are particularly at risk. Massive waves called tsunamis, which can reach 100 feet (30 m) or more in height, occasionally strike coastal areas on the Pacific Ocean.

Transportation. The first travelers on the Pacific may have been people from Southeast Asia who sailed to nearby islands, where they settled. By about A.D. 1000 most major islands, even the most remote, were inhabited. The islanders possessed the boatbuilding and navigating skills needed for very long voyages.

In 1513 Spanish explorer Vasco Núñez de Balboa sighted the ocean from the coast of Central America and called it the South Sea. Portuguese explorer Ferdinand Magellan renamed it the Pacific, which means peaceful. He sailed west across the Pacific from 1520 to 1521, and by the late 1700s, Europeans had explored and mapped most of the vast ocean.

From 1874 to 1875 scientists aboard the British vessel *Challenger* drew up samples of the deep Pacific floor. Mapping of the seafloor began in the 1930s and is still under way. During World War II the Pacific was the scene of large-scale sea and air combat, and ships and planes sunk in the fighting lie on the bottom near many tropical islands.

Since the end of World War II, trade throughout the Pacific region has increased dramatically. The Pacific nations of Asia now account for 40 percent of the foreign trade of the United States. **Maritime** traffic in the Pacific ports of Los Angeles and Long Beach, California, has begun to rival that of New York City. The boom in world trade on the Pacific Ocean has contributed to growth in the shipbuilding industry in Japan, South Korea, and Taiwan. *See also* AIR CURRENT AND WIND; ATLANTIC OCEAN.

maritime related to the sea or shipping

Panama Canal

The Panama Canal cuts southeastward across the Isthmus of Panama, a narrow strip of land in Central America that separates the Atlantic and Pacific Oceans. The 51-mile (82-km) canal, the world's busiest, offers ships an alternative to the 7,800-mile (12,550-km) journey around South America.

Construction of the Canal. A French company led by Ferdinand de Lesseps tried and failed to build a canal across Panama in the late 1800s. Soon after, the United States decided that such a canal would not only benefit commerce but would also speed the transfer of American warships between the Atlantic and Pacific Oceans in times of war. However, the Panama region was then a province of the country of Colombia, which refused to give the United States permission to build a canal.

In 1903, with the support of France and the United States, Panamanian rebels revolted against Colombia and won independence. The new government then signed a treaty allowing the United States to build, operate, and defend a canal.

Construction began in 1907, using steam shovels, railroads, and thousands of laborers to remove enormous amounts of rock and dirt from the canal route. Completed in 1913, the canal began full operation in 1920. Various improvements were made later, including the creation of Madden Lake to supply more water to the canal and the widening of the Gaillard Cut.

Conquering Disease

Tropical diseases such as yellow fever, malaria, and bubonic plague helped defeat the French attempt to build a canal in Panama during the 1800s. Thousands of workers died of disease. When the United States took over the project in 1904, Colonel William C. Gorgas assumed responsibility for health issues. Gorgas set up modern sanitation systems and launched an attack on the mosquitoes and rats that spread the diseases. His workers drained swamps and poured oil over mosquito-breeding areas, greatly lowering the death rate from disease.

The Route. On the Atlantic side the canal begins in Limón Bay near Cristobal, Panama. A short channel leads inland to the Gatun Locks, three high-walled concrete enclosures measuring 110 feet (34 m) wide and 1,000 feet (305 m) long. They can accommodate all but the largest ships, such as supertankers and large aircraft carriers. The locks raise or lower ships by 85 feet (26 m), the difference in water level between the Atlantic Ocean and Gatun Lake on the west side of the locks.

Once a ship is inside the lock, two massive gates close behind it. Canal engineers then allow water from Gatun Lake to flow into the lock and raise the ship to the level of the next lock, a step that takes anywhere from 8 to 15 minutes. Then the heavy gates at the far end of the lock open, allowing the ship to move forward into the next lock. Electric locomotives run on tracks on either side of the locks and help to pull and guide the ships through the narrow enclosures with attached cables.

Once out of the third lock, ships enter Gatun Lake, a large artificial lake created by the Gatun Dam. They thread their way past islands in the lake until they reach the Gaillard Cut, a channel dug through a highland section of the isthmus. Earth slides from the steep slopes on both sides of the cut are an ongoing problem, and workers must regularly dredge mud and rock from the channel to keep it open.

The Gaillard Cut ends at the Pedro Miguel Locks, which lower ships to the level of Miraflores Lake. Like Gatun Lake, Miraflores provides water for operating locks below it and serves as part of the canal as well. After crossing Miraflores, vessels reach the final two locks that take them down to the level of the Pacific Ocean—a drop that can vary by about 12.5 feet (almost 4 m) depending on the tides.

Beyond the locks, ships travel another 8 miles (13 km) through a channel to the end of the canal, just south of Panama City. From there they head out into the Bay of Panama and the open sea. In all, the voyage through the canal usually takes about eight hours.

A crew of about 8,000 workers keeps the canal operating 24 hours a day. On peak days up to 50 ships pass through. Even so, vessels must often wait in line at either end of the canal before being allowed to enter. About 70 percent of the traffic comes from or heads for a U.S. port. Ships passing through the canal carry such cargo as oil, iron, coal, lumber, steel, and foodstuffs. Military vessels also make up a large portion of the canal's traffic.

The Canal Today. For many years the Panama Canal served as a vital part of shipping lanes and as a strategic advantage for U.S. warships. However, the canal no longer plays such an important role in **maritime** traffic. Since World War II, the U.S. Navy has maintained strong fleets in both the Atlantic and Pacific Oceans, so passage through the canal is no longer essential. Although a steady stream of commercial traffic still passes through the canal, the use of oil pipelines, larger and faster supertankers, and **containerization** has taken away some of the canal's business.

In 1978 the United States agreed to return the canal and the territory around it to Panama in a gradual transfer of control ending on December 31, 1999. A second treaty guarantees that the canal will remain neutral and open to vessels of all nations even in times of war. *See also* CANALS; CONTAINERIZATION; ERIE CANAL; LESSEPS, FERDINAND DE; LOCKS; SUEZ CANAL.

maritime related to the sea or shipping

containerization method of shipping cargo in boxlike containers that can be transferred from one type of transportation to another

Pan American Airways

see Airline Industry.

Pan-American Highway

The Pan-American Highway is a system of roads that stretches from Alaska and Canada in North America to the tip of South America. It extends through the western United States and connects the capitals of 17 Latin American countries. Covering almost 30,000 miles (48,270 km), the highway is a continuous route with the exception of a 90-mile (145-km) tract of dense rain forest between Panama City and Colombia known as the Darien Gap.

The highway runs south from four points on the U.S.-Mexican border—Nogales in Arizona and El Paso, Eagle Pass, and Laredo in

Texas—through the mountains of Central America and into Panama. South of the Darien Gap, it resumes at Caracas, Venezuela, and continues to the capitals of Colombia, Ecuador, and Peru. Following the western coast of South America to Santiago, Chile, the highway turns east, crossing the Andes mountains to Buenos Aires, Argentina. An alternate route across the mountain range passes through La Paz, Bolivia, and runs southeast to Buenos Aires. Three separate branches of the highway link Buenos Aires to Paraguay, Uruguay, and Brazil.

The idea for an inter-American highway system to link North and South America by a network of roads was originally suggested in 1923 at the Fifth International Conference of American States. Work began in 1930. The pace of construction sped up during World War II to provide the U.S. military with a road to the Panama Canal, a vital route for moving ships, troops, and material between the Atlantic and Pacific Oceans. Various countries cooperated on the project. The United States contributed to the funding of specific parts of the highway in Central America, but Mexico assumed financial responsibility for the sections within its borders. Officially opened in 1963, the highway has played a key role in economic development in Latin America, particularly in the tourism industry. *See also* PANAMA CANAL; ROADS.

Parachutes

Parachutes slow the descent of people or equipment dropped from an airplane.

A parachute is a device used to slow the speed of a body moving through air. Its operation is based on the principle that air has mass and resists the movement of objects traveling through it. Air resistance, also called drag, increases with the surface area of the moving object. A parachute has a large canopy that provides enough drag to reduce the speed of the moving body.

The most common use of parachutes is to slow the descent of people or equipment dropped from an airplane. Parachutes can also brake vehicles traveling on the ground, such as high-speed automobiles or landing aircraft. In addition, spacecraft use parachutes to reduce their speed when returning to Earth.

An early version of the parachute may have been invented in China as early as the 1300s. The first successful jumps in Europe were made in France in the late 1700s by daredevils who leaped from trees, towers, and hot-air balloons. In the early 1800s a Frenchman, André Garnerin, jumped with a parachute of his own design from a height of 8,000 feet (2,438 m)—and lived.

In 1908 Leo Stevens of the United States invented the first manually operated parachute released from a pack by means of a rip cord. Parachutes were gradually adopted for use by military pilots. Major advances in design occurred during World War II, when pilots flew high-speed aircraft and air forces dropped large numbers of troops and equipment from the air.

The canopies of modern parachutes are usually made of nylon sewn together from wedge-shaped sections called gores. Nylon or Dacron lines—known as shroud lines or suspension lines—connect the canopy to heavy-duty straps. The straps are attached to a harness worn by the parachutist. The parachute and the lines must be folded carefully before being placed in a pack so that they will open properly when released. When the parachutist pulls a rip cord, the pack opens and releases the parachute.

In addition to the standard parachute, several other types are designed for special uses. Dome-shaped canopies are preferred for dropping equipment because they are highly stable in the air. Sport parachutes, usually rectangular, resemble an airplane's wing. This design allows the parachutist to control the forces of drag and **lift** and remain airborne for a long period of time. Such parachutes also feature steering lines to control the direction of gliding. *See also* AIRCRAFT; FLIGHT.

lift *force that pushes an aircraft (or other body) up and keeps it airborne*

Parades

A parade is a public procession held to celebrate victories, mark important occasions, honor heroes, and remember significant events of the past. During a parade, spectators line a route to watch participants pass by on foot or in vehicles that have been created or decorated for the occasion.

Some of the earliest parades took place in the ancient kingdom of Babylon in about 3000 B.C. They were designed to display the power and authority of the king. Early parades also celebrated military victories. Roman emperors arranged triumphal processions to honor Roman generals and soldiers who had won major battles and to exhibit captured prisoners and loot. Many parades still celebrate military and patriotic themes.

Although parades are held year-round in many parts of the world, most American parades are linked to public holidays such as New Year's Day, Memorial Day, the Fourth of July, and Thanksgiving. During these lively events, celebrities, marching bands, antique cars, and floats covered with flowers and other decorations join to create a colorful spectacle.

Two especially well-known parades, viewed by many people on television, are the Macy's Thanksgiving Day Parade in New York City and the Tournament of Roses Parade in Pasadena, California. The first features giant inflated balloons, and the second showcases floats decorated with thousands of flowers. Processions of lighted boats are becoming a popular tradition in many waterfront communities.

Parking

As the number of cars and trucks on the roads continues to increase, providing adequate parking space has become a pressing issue for many towns and cities. Stores need parking for their customers, and businesses need parking places for employees who drive to work. Schools, hospitals, and libraries all require parking for the people they serve. The types and amount of parking in a community can have an impact on traffic patterns and the local economy.

Most cities and towns provide parking **facilities** along the curbs of streets or in public lots. Parking may be free, or there may be a fee involved, usually based on the length of time a car will remain in the space. Drivers often pay the fee at a parking meter. Introduced in Oklahoma

facilities *something built or created to serve a particular function*

City in 1935, parking meters register the amount of time paid for and indicate when it has expired. In some places, an attendant stationed at the lot collects parking fees.

Many cities have begun to limit the amount of parking on the street to improve traffic flow. They may provide multistory parking garages, either above or below street level, to accommodate drivers. However, these lots are expensive to build and maintain.

Many parking lots and garages are privately owned. In addition to short-term parking, they may offer daily or weekly rates. Airports, bus stations, railroad stations, and harbors also provide short- and long-term parking for motorists boarding another form of transport.

mass transit system of public transportation in an urban area

In the suburbs, where **mass transit** services are limited, people rely heavily on cars for transportation. As a result, suburban shopping malls and office parks are often surrounded by acres of parking lots. *See also* AIRPORTS; AUTOMOBILES, EFFECTS OF; COMMUTING; DRIVING; HARBORS AND PORTS; MALLS; MOTELS; RAILWAY STATIONS.

Passenger Trains

see *Passengers; Railway Trains, Types of.*

Passengers

Throughout history people have traveled as passengers in various forms of transportation. The vehicles that carried them have ranged from simple carts and flatboats to steam-powered ships and railroads to buses equipped with gasoline or diesel engines to the jet planes of modern times. Over the years, the speed and capacity of the forms of transportation available to passengers have increased enormously.

Travel in ancient times was usually difficult and dangerous. Except for walking, it also could be very costly. As a result, few people journeyed beyond their immediate region. Not until the mid-1700s did passenger travel become fairly common, largely because of the development of new and more efficient forms of transport. Today, ships, trains, buses, planes, and a variety of other vehicles provide transportation for millions of passengers around the world on a daily basis.

Boats and Ships.
As long ago as 6000 B.C., boats carried passengers up and down the Nile River in ancient Egypt. Although most early ships were meant for carrying cargo, travelers could often pay for passage on them.

Travel by ship grew significantly in the 1600s, when thousands of colonists sailed to America. By the early 1800s, the demand for **transatlantic** travel had greatly increased, and shipping companies began regularly scheduled service on sailing vessels called packet ships. By the mid-1800s steamships provided most of the passenger service on ocean crossings.

transatlantic relating to crossing the Atlantic Ocean

As the number of passengers increased, shipping companies built larger and faster ships. By the early 1900s, they had launched numerous ocean liners, giant ships that could carry thousands of passengers. Most offered luxurious accommodations. Smaller ships continued to carry

Passengers board an Amtrak train in Wilmington, Delaware. Today rail service accounts for only a small portion of intercity travel in the United States.

passengers, generally immigrants, who could not afford to travel on ocean liners.

By the mid-1900s air travel began to lure passengers away from ships. Unable to compete, many ocean liners were taken out of service. In the 1980s, however, passenger travel on ships experienced a rebirth with the development of the cruise industry. Today, ships ranging in size from small yachts to huge luxury liners offer vacation cruises throughout the world.

Another form of passenger service on ships is provided by ferries. Ferries have been used to carry people and their vehicles across rivers, harbors, lakes, and other bodies of water for hundreds of years. In some places, they remain an important means of passenger travel.

Stagecoaches. Horse-drawn carts and wagons carried travelers on overland routes for centuries. The desire for greater comfort gradually led to the development of various types of enclosed coaches, supported by springs to provide a smoother ride. Horse-drawn coaches appeared in the 1400s in Europe, where they were used almost exclusively by monarchs and wealthy aristocrats. By the 1600s coaches began to carry mail and passengers between towns. They became known as stagecoaches, because they traveled in stages, stopping at various points along their routes. The first long-distance stage line, established about 1670, ran between London and Edinburgh, Scotland.

In colonial America, stagecoach lines were established in the mid-1700s to link eastern cities such as Boston, Philadelphia, and New York. However, passenger coaches did not become common until the 1800s, when road conditions and the comfort of the vehicle improved. Between 1800 and 1840, stagecoaches provided the only means of long-distance passenger service in the United States.

Stagecoaches came in various sizes, with seating for between 6 and 16 passengers. They made regular stops at taverns and inns, where the passengers could find both food and lodging. By the 1880s stagecoach service had largely been replaced by the development of railroads.

Railroads. The rise of railroads helped revolutionize passenger travel, offering fast and safe transportation over short and long distances. The first rail passenger cars were little more than stagecoaches with wheels that could run on railroad tracks. Within a few years, however, specially designed railway cars offered a degree of comfort and luxury previously unknown in passenger travel.

The first scheduled passenger rail line in the United States, begun in the 1830s, ran 136 miles (219 km) between Charleston and Hamburg in South Carolina. By 1850 the nation had more than 9,000 miles (14,480 km) of track, and trains carried tens of thousands of passengers. The completion of a **transcontinental** railroad line in 1869 made it possible to travel from New York to San Francisco in only six days.

Between the mid-1800s and early 1900s, the railroads greatly expanded their routes and upgraded passenger service. They offered features such as meals and sleeping accommodations in specially designed dining and sleeping cars. Improvements to engines and heating and lighting systems helped create a smoother and more comfortable ride.

Rail passenger service reached its height in the United States in the 1920s. Thereafter, the railroads began losing business to motor vehicles and airplanes. By the 1960s passenger services on railroads had declined dramatically. Many railroad companies went out of business or shifted their focus to freight.

Modern passenger railroads account for less than 1 percent of total intercity passenger traffic in the United States. However, in Europe and other parts of the world, railroads remain an important form of passenger travel.

Subways and Light Rail. Underground railway systems, better known as subways or metros, provide another method of moving passengers along a fixed route. Subways were built in urban areas in Europe and the United States beginning in the late 1800s. Automatic subway trains run by computers appeared in the 1970s. They usually have one crew member aboard to operate computer controls and handle any mechanical problems that arise.

Light rail systems—including modern versions of streetcars and trolleys, monorails, and cable cars—also carry passengers in cities. After a long period of decline, these primarily electric-powered forms of transportation are gaining favor today as a way to lessen traffic congestion and the pollution of motor vehicles.

Buses and Automobiles. First developed in the late 1800s, motorized buses competed for many years with streetcars and trolleys as a form of passenger transportation in urban areas. Because buses did not require tracks, their routes could be changed easily. By the 1970s streetcars and trolleys had nearly disappeared and buses remained a popular method of commuter travel, carrying passengers within cities and between cities and suburbs. School buses, found in nearly every community in the United States, transport students on regular routes between home and school and to special events.

transcontinental *extending across a continent*

New Life for Old Ships

With the decline of ocean liner travel in the mid-1900s, shipping companies tried to find new uses for their huge and costly vessels. Some ships, like the *Queen Mary,* were moored permanently at ports and became floating hotels and tourist attractions. Some were retired from service and scrapped. Others were modernized and converted to cruise ships. One of the largest cruise ships, the SS *Norway,* began life as an ocean liner, the SS *France.* The ship once carried passengers across the cold North Atlantic Ocean but now takes vacationers on cruises in the sunny Caribbean.

Intercity and tour buses are designed for long-distance travel. Most of these vehicles are equipped with air-conditioning, onboard restrooms, comfortable high-back seats, luggage racks, individual reading lights, and a separate storage compartment.

No other form of transportation in the United States is as popular as the automobile. Cars offer passengers greater convenience and flexibility than buses, trains, and other kinds of public transportation, which move according to fixed schedules and routes. Taxis and limousines in urban and suburban areas are the only automobiles generally used to carry paying passengers. However, the widespread ownership of private cars has had an enormous impact on transportation in the United States, causing a serious reduction in passenger traffic on buses and trains.

Aircraft. Europeans pioneered airline passenger service in 1919, when a British company began flying passengers between London and Paris. The United States introduced passenger service soon after.

At first air travel was a novelty. But as planes became larger and more powerful, passenger traffic increased steadily. By the late 1930s airlines offered comfortable seating, quiet cabins, in-flight meals, and onboard bathrooms. Most passengers on these airlines were either wealthy individuals or business travelers.

Since the introduction of jet passenger service in the late 1950s, the number of airplane passengers and flights has grown dramatically. Thousands of flights now depart from and arrive at airports around the world each day, and airlines carry billions of people each year. Many airline passengers are vacationers, and jet travel has helped make tourism an important worldwide industry. Today regional and commuter jets can fly distances of up to 1,000 miles (1,610 km), and the U.S. Federal Aviation Administration expects passenger traffic on these aircraft to increase at a faster pace than that of larger carriers. *See also* AIRLINE INDUSTRY; AIRPORTS; AMTRAK; AUTOMOBILES, HISTORY OF; BUSES; CARTS, CARRIAGES, AND WAGONS;

Thousands of flights arrive and depart at airports around the world each day. O'Hare International Airport in Chicago remains one of the busiest passenger airports.

COMMUTING; CRUISE SHIPS; CUNARD LINE; EURAIL SYSTEM; FERRIES; HIGH-SPEED TRAINS; HORSES; JET PLANES; LIGHT RAIL SYSTEMS; OCEAN LINERS; PUBLIC TRANSPORTATION; RAILROADS, HISTORY OF; SHIPS AND BOATS, TYPES OF; STAGECOACHES; STEAMBOATS; TOURISM; TRANSCONTINENTAL RAILROAD; TRAVEL INDUSTRY; URBAN TRANSPORTATION.

Passports and Visas

For hundreds of years, people have carried various types of documents as a means of identification and protection while traveling from one country to another. Only in relatively modern times, however, have national governments required official papers for foreign travel. The two most important of these documents are passports and visas.

Passports.   A passport is a document issued by a government that identifies its holder as a citizen of that nation. It contains basic information about the individual, including name, date and place of birth, and nationality. A United States passport also requests that other countries permit the holder to travel freely and safely within their borders and to extend "all lawful aid and protection" to the individual while he or she is under their jurisdiction. Countries that do not have diplomatic relations with one another will not acknowledge each other's passports and their terms. In such cases, travel to those places may be banned or restricted. If a nation is going through a period of political unrest, terrorism, or some other condition that could make travel difficult or dangerous, foreign governments may issue a travel advisory to their citizens.

Although passports are generally needed for travel abroad, some nations have signed agreements that allow citizens of other countries to visit without these documents. Citizens of the United States, for example, do not need a passport to enter Canada, Mexico, and most of the Caribbean islands. An official identification card allows citizens of the European Union to travel, work, and reside in any of its member states.

Passports in the United States are issued by the State Department. To obtain a passport, a person first submits an application, which is available from passport agencies, state or federal court buildings, and post offices. The application must be accompanied by proof of identity and citizenship, two recent photos, and a fee. U.S. passports are valid for ten years for individuals 18 years and older, but citizens under age 18 must renew their passports every five years.

Visas.   A visa is a stamp or printed endorsement placed in a passport by officials of a foreign government. It certifies that those officials have examined and approved the passport, and it specifies the conditions under which the holder of the passport can travel to that country. Visa applications are available at a foreign country's embassy or consulate, a travel agency, or a visa service.

There are several types of visas. Transit visas allow travelers to pass through, but not stay in, a country. Tourist visas permit individuals to visit a country for a certain period of time. People who plan to study in another country often need a student visa, while those who want to work or conduct business abroad must usually obtain a work visa or

Border guards at the Berlin Wall in Germany checked tourists' passports when Berlin was a divided city that belonged to different nations.

business visa. To live in a foreign country for an extended period, a person generally needs a residence visa.

Many countries no longer require tourist visas. For example, U.S. citizens do not need such documents to travel to many countries in Western Europe. However, tourists must obtain visas to visit many nations in other parts of the world, and most countries require visas for other types of travel. *See also* TOURISM.

People Movers

People movers are driverless, electric-powered vehicles, consisting of single- or multi-car trains that travel on a fixed guideway, or track. The guideways may be located at ground level, aboveground, or underground. In some areas people movers have become a practical alternative to automobiles and other modes of transportation.

At times of peak ridership, people movers can be operated with less than 60 seconds of headway—the time between the departure of one vehicle and the arrival of the next—and they can carry up to 25,000 passengers an hour in one direction. Capable of reaching speeds of about 55 miles (88 km) per hour, people movers offer precisely controlled speed, acceleration, and deceleration, providing a safe, smooth, and reliable ride.

Most people movers in the United States are located in airports, amusement parks, and zoos. However, the cities of Miami and Detroit also use them to transport passengers to downtown areas. In other parts of the world, people movers travel longer distances and play a more significant role in **mass transit.** For example, the SkyTrain in Vancouver, Canada, makes 110,000 trips per day and carries 35 million passengers annually, and the VAL System in Lille, France, transports 230,000 passengers every workday.

mass transit *system of public transportation in an urban area*

Moving sidewalks, another type of people mover, consist of a continuous rubber belt on rollers or jointed sections linked together. Similar to escalators, these moving ramps can carry passengers horizontally or at slight inclines. Moving sidewalks are used mainly in activity centers, such as airports, that have a great deal of foot traffic. *See also* Elevators and Escalators; Light Rail Systems; Urban Transportation.

Petroleum

see Energy.

Pilots, Aircraft

Piloting an aircraft requires special skills, knowledge, and training. It also demands continual practice and study to keep up with changing technology and flight procedures and to maintain the proficiency needed to remain a licensed pilot. More than 500,000 people in the United States have a pilot's license. About 100,000 of them are licensed to work for major airlines; the rest are qualified to fly small private and commercial planes and military aircraft.

Licensing of Pilots. All pilots in the United States must be licensed by the FAA (Federal Aviation Administration). The FAA establishes the minimum requirements for obtaining and keeping a license to fly a plane, known officially as a flight certificate.

There are several types of flight certificates, each with its own special conditions. A basic requirement for all pilots is the ability to understand, read, and speak English. Accepted worldwide as the international language of aviation, English is used to give all air traffic control instructions and other flight information. People who wish to acquire any type of flight certificate must also pass a physical examination to ensure that they are in good health.

Anyone who wants to take flight training must obtain a student pilot certificate. Student pilots must be at least 16 years of age. They may not fly a plane that carries passengers, and they cannot transport cargo for money.

A private pilot certificate allows a pilot to carry passengers and property, but not for money. To obtain this certificate, a person must be at least 17 years old and have a minimum of 40 hours of flying experience, including 20 hours flying alone without an instructor.

A commercial pilot certificate confers the right to carry passengers or property for money but does not qualify the pilot to fly for large commercial airlines. The minimum age requirement for this type of pilot certificate is 18, and individuals must have at least 250 hours of flying time, including a certain number of hours flying at night and in different types of aircraft.

To work for major airlines, a pilot needs an airline transport certificate. In addition to a minimum age requirement of 23 and at least 1,500 hours of flying

This pilot sits in the cockpit of an airplane before an air show demonstration. More than 500,000 people in the United States have a pilot's license.

time (including 100 hours at night), this certificate requires individuals to have experience as a pilot or copilot in command of an aircraft and to complete a course on flying with electronic navigational instruments.

Aerial Flips and Turns

In recent years, fewer airline pilots have begun their careers as military fighter pilots. As a result, many of them have no experience with mishaps—such as rolling over in the air—that occur in combat but rarely in commercial aviation. For safety reasons, airline training programs have introduced special simulators that place pilots in extreme situations. The simulators tilt and sway to create the sensation of an airplane rolling steeply or turning upside down. To return to level flight, pilots learn special maneuvers—such as banking the plane very sharply—which they may have seen only in old combat movies.

aerodynamics branch of science that deals with the motion of air and the effects of such motion on planes and other objects

meteorology scientific study of weather and weather forecasting

maneuver series of changes in course

aeronautics the science of flight

Flight Training.   Learning to fly involves instruction both on the ground and in the air. While on the ground, pilots take various courses in **aerodynamics,** navigation, **meteorology,** and the rules and regulations of aviation. Flight instruction consists of many hours of actually flying an aircraft, both under the guidance of a certified flight instructor and solo. At advanced levels, some flight instruction may be carried out in a simulator—a machine laid out like the cockpit of a plane with controls that function like those in a real aircraft.

Pilots must learn many flight **maneuvers,** including how to taxi on a runway, take off, and land. They also receive instruction in navigating with the aircraft's instruments rather than with ground observation. As training progresses and flying time increases, pilots must demonstrate their skills and knowledge through written and flight examinations. The level of skill and expertise, along with accumulated flying time and experience, determines their qualifications for receiving the different types of flight certificates issued by the FAA.

Learning to fly can be quite expensive. The cost of obtaining a flight certificate can range from $2,000 or $3,000 to well over $15,000, depending on the type of certificate. Many people begin learning to fly at local airports and flight schools. In addition, more than 30 colleges and universities in the United States offer flight instruction and courses on **aeronautics.**

Many pilots get their start in the military. All branches of the U.S. armed forces have training programs for pilots, and many commercial pilots receive their initial training in the military. In some countries, the major airlines have programs to train their pilots as well.

Unlike a driver's license, a flight certificate has no expiration date. But keeping a pilot's license requires recent flight experience as well as up-to-date knowledge of aviation regulations. All pilots undergo periodic flight reviews that test their flying skills and understanding of current operating and flight rules. The requirements for these reviews vary according to the type of flight certificate and planes flown. Pilots who fail to demonstrate adequate skills and knowledge are usually required to take additional flight instruction and courses. *See also* AIRLINE INDUSTRY; AVIATION; CAREERS IN TRANSPORTATION; FAA (FEDERAL AVIATION ADMINISTRATION); FLIGHT; NAVIGATION.

Pioneer 10 and 11

see Space Exploration.

Pipelines

A pipeline is a system of pipes used to transport liquids, gases, and certain other substances over long distances. Water, petroleum, and natural gas are the most common materials in pipelines, but slurries—finely crushed solid materials, such as coal, that are suspended in liquid—also travel by pipeline.

The Trans-Alaska Oil Pipeline, approximately 800 miles (1,290 km) long, crosses two mountain ranges and 34 rivers and streams. It runs through Alaska from Prudhoe Bay in the north to Valdez in the south.

conduit *channel or pipe for carrying a liquid or gas*

aqueduct *artificial channel for carrying water*

Pipelines play an important role in modern transportation. Large networks of **conduits** carry virtually all the water delivered to homes and businesses in urban and suburban areas, as well as the sewage and wastewater carried away to treatment plants. Pipelines also deliver most of the natural gas used by individuals. Much of the oil and other petroleum products sent over long distances on land also travels in pipelines.

History of Pipelines.   Humans have used pipes for thousands of years to carry water for drinking and irrigation. The ancient Chinese, Romans, and Persians all built pipelines to bring water to their cities. The Roman system of conduits and **aqueducts** was perhaps the most extensive in the ancient world. As early as the 400s B.C., the Chinese also used bamboo pipes to transport natural gas.

Early pipelines operated by the force of gravity. The conduits were laid on a gradual incline and the water simply flowed downhill. An important advance in technology came about in 1582 when the city of London installed pumps to help push water through its system of pipelines. Other improvements occurred in the 1700s and 1800s with the introduction of iron and steel pipes. These materials made pipelines stronger and more practical for long distances.

During the mid-1800s pipelines became important for distributing water in the United States. The country's first gas pipeline was built in 1825; the first oil pipeline opened in 1865. Pipeline construction expanded rapidly during the 1900s.

A variety of developments since the mid-1900s have made pipelines one of the safest, cheapest, and most efficient means of transporting certain products. Major pipelines can be found all over the world. Some of the longest are in Russia, including a 4,000-mile (6,436-km) gas line that runs from Siberia to Western Europe. The United States possesses the most extensive system of pipelines in the world, with about 200,000 miles (321,800 km) of major pipelines and hundreds of thousands of miles of smaller ones.

Design and Operation. Pipeline systems are designed very much like railroad networks. Smaller pipes called gathering lines carry the substance from its place of origin, such as an oil well or water reservoir, to larger conduits called trunk lines.

Trunk lines may lead to a variety of locations. They take natural gas to processing centers, and from there the gas is pumped through smaller pipes—called distribution lines—directly to customers. Petroleum travels through trunk lines either to refineries or to shipping points, where it is loaded onto ships, trucks, or railroad cars. After petroleum is refined into gasoline or other products, a conduit called a product pipeline carries the product to the places where it will be used.

Transporting substances through a pipeline requires more than just pipes. As a gas or liquid moves through a pipeline, it is slowed down by **friction.** Pumping stations are located at regular intervals along pipelines, and the pumps supply pressure that keeps the substance flowing. The distance between these stations can range from 30 to 150 miles (48 to 241 km), depending on the material being transported and the terrain. Conduits running through hilly areas require more closely spaced pumps than those running over flat land. Pipelines also have various types of valves to direct and control the flow of a substance. In regions with very cold climates, some type of heating element may be used to keep liquids in the pipes from freezing.

Most pipelines consist of steel pipes welded together, but aluminum, concrete, iron, and even plastic may also be used. The pipes range in size from about 2 inches (5 cm) to 48 inches (122 cm) in diameter. They are usually laid underground to protect them from damage and to prevent spills that could harm the environment. Metal pipes are coated with a special type of paint or wrapped in a protective material as a safeguard against **corrosion.** Conduits that carry water usually have some type of plastic or cement lining to prevent rusting, which can harm the water quality.

Pipelines sometimes carry several substances at the same time. The substances are pumped one after the other in "batches" from 15 to 20 miles (24 to 32 km) long. The most valuable materials are kept separate to avoid being **contaminated** by other substances. Near the end of the pipeline, a special device measures the differences in weight of the materials to determine where one batch ends and the next begins. Another way to separate the batches is to place an inflated rubber ball between them. *See also* AQUEDUCTS; TRANS-ALASKA PIPELINE.

friction *force that produces a resistance to motion*

corrosion *process of wearing away gradually, usually by chemical erosion*

contaminate *to pollute*

Piracy

Pirates have been known by many names—buccaneers, sea rovers, freebooters, and corsairs. From ancient times until the mid-1800s, they roamed the seas in search of ships carrying valuable cargo. Although pirate attacks are no longer common, mariners in small craft in certain areas are still at risk.

The 1958 Geneva Convention on the High Seas defines piracy as an illegal act of violence or theft committed outside the territory of any nation by the people aboard one vessel against another vessel. This definition applies to both ships and aircraft. Acts carried out as part of law enforcement or for political reasons in times of war or rebellion, however, are not considered piracy. The theft of a vessel and its cargo, robbery or kidnapping of the passengers and crew—and even murder—fall under the general heading of piracy.

In ancient times piracy was widespread in the Mediterranean Sea, the home of many early seafaring peoples. When pirate attacks began to pose a serious threat to Roman shipping, Rome led several large-scale military campaigns to destroy the enemy bases. During the Middle Ages, pirates known as corsairs thrived along the North African coasts of Tunisia and Algeria. Their raids in pursuit of loot and slaves took them as far north as the English Channel. Not until the early 1800s did the navies of Europe and the United States bring these Barbary pirates under control.

galleon large sailing ship used for war and trade

After the discovery of the Americas, the Caribbean Sea attracted adventurers of all sorts. Many of them hoped to capture Spanish **galleons** transporting huge amounts of gold and silver from the colonies in Central and South America to Europe. From the 1500s to the 1800s, English, French, and Dutch pirates preyed not only on shipping but also on coastal settlements.

During this period many privateers also roamed the high seas in search of treasure ships. They differed from pirates, although their actions were often similar. While pirates operated outside the law, privateers sailing in privately owned ships were authorized by their governments to attack the vessels of enemy nations. Many countries hired privateers for warfare, and when the fighting ended, some privateers continued their activities as pirates. On the other side, pirates sometimes took advantage of the frequent wars among the European nations to become privateers.

Piracy was common in Asia and other parts of the world as well. Between the 1300s and 1600s, traders based in Japan actively engaged in piracy in Chinese waters if they disagreed with the terms of trade or if they were not granted entry to particular ports. At one time there were so many pirate communities along the Persian Gulf that the area came to be known as the Pirate Coast.

By the mid-1800s large-scale piracy had been eliminated as a result of the presence of strong navies in most waters. Larger shipping vessels and the recognition of piracy as an international crime also played a role in decreasing pirate attacks. However, piracy still occurs on a small scale in Southeast Asia and elsewhere. *See also* CRIME; HIJACKING.

Police

see Crime.

Pollution and Transportation

Throughout most of human history, transportation relied on sources of power that were clean and nonpolluting, such as muscle power, animal power, or wind. However, that changed with the development of fuel-burning engines in the 1800s. From the time that steam engines were first mounted on locomotives and carriages, transportation has played a role in environmental pollution.

Transportation is one of the leading causes of air pollution in industrialized nations. Traffic conditions in Mexico City contribute to the area's severe pollution problem.

pollutant *something that contaminates the environment*

Today transportation-related activities have a major impact on the environment. Hundreds of millions of automobiles pump tons of **pollutants** into the air every day. Trucks, trains, ships, and aircraft contribute to air pollution as well. In addition, transportation plays a part in water pollution when trucks, ships, or trains spill oil, chemicals, and other waste materials. Some vehicles, including jet planes and subways, create noise pollution with the loud sounds they produce.

Because of the various health hazards associated with pollution, governments and organizations devote a great deal of time, money, and other resources to reducing it and cleaning up the environment. A large portion of their energies is focused on transportation because of its key role in pollution problems.

Air Pollution. Transportation is a leading cause of air pollution in the United States and other industrialized nations. Automobiles, aircraft, ships, and trains all burn **fossil fuels,** which generate airborne pollutants such as carbon monoxide, carbon dioxide, and hydrocarbons (compounds of carbon and hydrogen).

fossil fuel *coal, petroleum, or other fuel formed from prehistoric plants and animals*

Some of these pollutants are harmful to human health, causing or aggravating heart problems, respiratory ailments, and lung disease. A number of them affect the environment. Scientists warn that a growing concentration of carbon dioxide in the atmosphere is a factor in global warming, a slow increase in average annual temperatures. Another danger comes from chlorofluorocarbons (CFCs), a pollutant produced by air-conditioning units that were installed in older motor vehicles. CFCs damage the ozone layer of the atmosphere, a region that shields all life on Earth against harmful **radiation** from the sun.

radiation *energy given off in waves or particles*

emissions *substances discharged into the air*

Transportation-related air pollution has been a problem for many years, but only recently have governments taken steps to reduce it. The first federal regulations to control motor vehicle **emissions** in the United States were passed in 1965. Since 1975 most American-made cars have had devices called catalytic converters, which eliminate some pollutants. Laws have also restricted the use of lead compounds in gasoline. Automobiles using unleaded gasoline burn fuel more efficiently and cleanly, reducing the amount of pollutants. In addition, the government now requires car manufacturers to install air conditioners that do not release CFCs. Both a 1989 international agreement and the U.S. Clean Air Act of 1990 put programs in place to phase out the use of CFCs in the early 2000s.

Many states have devised programs to combat transportation-related air pollution. In the 1990s California and a number of eastern states approved regulations requiring automakers to include a certain percentage of vehicles that meet very strict standards in their product lines. Some of these vehicles were hybrids featuring electric motors and gasoline engines. Others were driven by nonpolluting fuel cells.

Buses and highway trucks, which generally run on diesel, are subject to air-quality standards as well. These requirements, however, are not as strict as those imposed on cars. In 1995 the Environmental Protection Agency (EPA), the California Air Resources Board (ARB), and heavy-duty vehicle manufacturers agreed to reduce nitrogen oxide emissions from new trucks and buses by half.

Government regulations also limit the pollutants released by aircraft. Emissions of hydrocarbons from airplane engines have been regulated since 1984. Standards for carbon dioxide and other substances were added in 1997. Despite such progress, transportation-related air pollution remains a very serious problem throughout the world.

Water Pollution. Most transportation-related water pollution results from the release of products such as oil, chemicals, and waste materials carried in water or land vehicles. Often, such substances are released accidentally into the environment. But sometimes they are dumped deliberately into oceans, lakes, and rivers. These pollutants can damage supplies of drinking water and harm or kill various species of marine plants and animals.

Oil spills are the best-known example of transportation-related water pollution. Each year thousands of accidental spills occur around the world, discharging millions of gallons of oil into marine environments. Most of these spills are small, involving only a few gallons of oil, but accidents can produce large-scale pollution. The most highly publicized oil spill in the United States occurred in 1989 when the ship *Exxon Valdez* released nearly 11 million gallons of oil off the coast of Alaska.

Land-based vehicles can contribute to water pollution as well when they spill chemicals and various toxic substances. Such spills generally result from accidents involving trucks or trains. The substances released can cause immediate danger to people near the scene of the accident. They may also flow into streams, harming marine life, or into the ground, **contaminating** underground water supplies.

Federal regulations in the United States spell out proper procedures for the handling and transportation of all hazardous materials. These rules have reduced the chances of accidental spills or leakage. The Oil Pollution Act of 1990 required new oil tankers to be built with double hulls that are less likely to leak in case of an accident.

Smog

People in urban areas sometimes notice a hazy cloud of polluted air overhead. Known as smog, from the words *smoke* and *fog,* this type of air pollution can result from a concentration of automobile exhaust fumes and emissions from factories. Certain weather conditions can create a warm layer of air over a city, trapping pollutants. Mountain ranges also prevent emissions from escaping. When the pollutants from burning gasoline are exposed to sunshine, they form hazardous gases that can irritate the eyes, nose, and throat. Heavy smog can be dangerous for people with respiratory problems. Despite measures to reduce exhaust from cars and industry, smog is still a serious problem in some cities.

contaminate to pollute

Water pollution also comes from the deliberate pumping of wastes into the oceans. Many ships routinely dump garbage, sewage, and other wastes far out at sea. Over the long term, such dumping can be very harmful to ocean environments. An international treaty signed by many nations in 1988 prohibits the dumping of plastics in the ocean, and a U.S. law passed in 1992 banned all ocean dumping.

Noise Pollution. Transportation also plays a leading role in noise pollution. Persistent loud noise from jet planes, subways, and heavy traffic can cause stress, irritability, hearing loss, and even heart attacks. Many communities in the United States have attempted to reduce noise pollution by shifting air flight patterns, using rubber tires on subways, erecting noise barriers between highways and residential areas, and adopting regulations banning car horns and other loud noises in certain places. *See also* ACCIDENTS; AUTOMOBILES, EFFECTS OF; ENERGY; HAZARDOUS MATERIALS, TRANSPORT OF; HEALTH ISSUES; NOISE CONTROL; RAILROADS, HISTORY OF; REGULATION OF TRANSPORTATION; SHIPS AND BOATS, SAFETY OF; TANKERS.

Pony Express

The Pony Express was a mail service that started as a publicity stunt but became a legend of the American West. During its 18 months in operation, young men riding fast horses set new speed records for carrying mail between St. Joseph, Missouri, and Sacramento, California.

In the mid-1800s mail usually traveled between the eastern United States and California by stagecoach on a slow, winding route through the southern part of the country. A one-way trip took more than three weeks. The owners of a freight-hauling firm thought that they could make the trip faster by following a central route. Their goal was to win the profitable government contract for carrying mail.

The company purchased swift Indian ponies and hired lightweight riders, many of them teenage boys. They were to follow the route of the stagecoach line as far west as Salt Lake City. From there the riders would have to establish a new trail through Utah and Nevada to arrive in California. Stations were built about 10 to 15 miles (16 to 24 km) apart in the regions that were not on the route of the stagecoach service.

On April 3, 1860, the Pony Express was launched. Carrying mail in a saddlebag, a rider raced from station to station with two minutes allowed for changing horses at each stop. After he had covered about 75 miles (121 km), he turned the mail over to the next rider. This relay system reduced the time required to transport mail from Missouri to California to ten days.

Riders were in the saddle most of the day and night. They traveled in all kinds of weather over rugged terrain. Despite hardships and hazards, the Pony Express was highly successful at getting the mail through, once achieving a record delivery time of six days. But the completion of the first **transcontinental** telegraph line on October 24, 1861, brought instant communication, eliminating the need for the Pony Express. Moreover, the mail service had been so costly to operate that the company running it was ruined.

transcontinental extending across a continent

Postal Service

Postal services collect and deliver mail and packages. In nearly all countries, these systems are administered by the national government. Before the invention of the telegraph and telephone, postal services provided the fastest and most reliable means of communication over long distances. Despite the rapid growth of electronic communications in recent times, the public continues to rely heavily on the world's postal services. In most cases, they are a convenient and inexpensive way of sending written communications and goods.

History of Postal Services. The earliest postal system was probably developed by the Egyptians around 2000 B.C., followed by the Chinese about a thousand years later. Ancient postal services consisted of messengers who carried government communications to and from various parts of a kingdom. The Persians and Romans both maintained extensive networks of well-built roads with relay stations where messengers could rest, take a new horse, or pass their message to a new rider.

Postal systems in Europe nearly disappeared after the fall of Rome around A.D. 500, but they emerged again during the Renaissance as privately owned companies. For instance, the Taxis family of Vienna built a flourishing postal network that served the Holy Roman Empire from the 1500s to the mid-1800s. However, the rise of national governments put most European postal services under government control by the 1700s.

Britain introduced many new features to improve service. During the 1700s the British postal system began carrying mail in stagecoaches. In the 1800s it adopted the proposals of a British educator named Rowland Hill to use envelopes and prepaid stamps and to charge for delivery by weight instead of distance. International mail came under a uniform system with the signing of the General Postal Union Treaty in 1875.

The speed and convenience of mail delivery increased with new forms of transportation—railroads, steamships, and airplanes. The first

Airmail service between New York and Washington, D.C., began as early as 1918. Regular airmail flights across the United States started in 1924.

Postal Timeline

Most people take things like postage stamps and ZIP codes for granted, but they are only recent additions to the history of the U.S. Postal Service.

1639	First post office set up in a Boston tavern
1775	American postal system established by Continental Congress
1847	Postage stamps
1855	Registered letter service
1864	First postal money orders
1924	First transcontinental airmail service
1963	Five-digit ZIP codes
1977	Next-day Express Mail
1983	Nine-digit ZIP codes

transcontinental *extending across a continent*

regular international air service began in 1919 between London and Paris, and airmail across the Atlantic Ocean became available in the late 1930s. Global airmail service expanded after World War II.

Postal services also benefited from new mechanical devices that sorted, postmarked, and canceled mail—and even read addresses on envelopes. These machines took over jobs that postal workers once performed by hand, allowing postal systems to speed up delivery and deal with huge increases in the volume of mail.

Postal Service in the United States. Mail service in colonial America dates from 1639 and was under the control of the British government. In 1775 in the spirit of rebellion, the colonies took over their postal services, and the Continental Congress named Benjamin Franklin the first postmaster general of the United States. In 1789 the nation's 75 post offices became part of the U.S. Post Office Department.

The department faced a new challenge in covering the huge expanses of western land that the United States acquired and settled. From 1860 to 1861 a private service, the Pony Express, carried mail from St. Joseph, Missouri, to Sacramento, California. Relay riders on horseback covered the trip of 2,000 miles (3,218 km) in just ten days. However, the Pony Express was replaced by the telegraph network that linked the continent by 1861.

In the mid-1860s free home delivery of mail began in many American cities. The railroads, which had been transporting letters and packages to post offices for decades, began serving the public directly from railroad post office cars. The boom in railroad building after the Civil War brought greater efficiency to the postal delivery system.

In 1902 home delivery became available for people living in rural areas. In 1913 the U.S. Post Office introduced parcel post for sending packages. Airmail between New York and Washington, D.C., began as early as 1918, and regular **transcontinental** airmail flights started in 1924.

Since its creation, the U.S. Post Office had operated under the direct control of the federal government and received public money to help cover its costs and keep the price of postage low. In 1970, however, the Federal Postal Reorganization Act changed the status of the post office from a department in the federal government to a partly independent agency. Known as the United States Postal Service (USPS), the new agency was allowed to raise the price of stamps to replace its government funding, and it finally showed a profit in 1983.

Efforts to automate tasks have helped the USPS streamline its operations, improve service, and save money. New developments have included ZIP codes, presorted bulk mail, bar codes, optical scanning devices, and Express Mail service. These changes have enabled the postal service to compete with private package delivery companies and other new forms of communication, such as E-mail.

The USPS currently delivers more than 198 billion pieces of mail a year to about 130 million homes and businesses—about 650 million pieces of mail a day. To get the job done, it operates about 38,000 post offices and employs more than 775,000 people, making it the nation's largest employer other than the military. The USPS also maintains its own fleets of trucks and airplanes. *See also* COMMUNICATION SYSTEMS; PONY EXPRESS; ROMAN ROADS.

Public Transportation

Millions of people around the world rely on public transportation each day to get from one place to another. They use a variety of transit systems, including buses, subways, trains, light rail systems, airplanes, and ferries—all of which offer scheduled passenger service to the general public.

History. The roots of modern public transportation go back to the early 1800s, when horse-drawn streetcars that ran along tracks appeared in urban areas in Europe and the United States. New York City became a pioneer in public transportation in the 1820s and 1830s, with licensed horse-drawn coaches called omnibuses that carried passengers on regular routes along major streets. Soon other U.S. cities had fleets of omnibuses as well, and they provided competition to streetcars. At about the same time, early railways in Great Britain began offering passenger service between certain destinations.

After the invention of the steam engine, steam and electricity gradually replaced horses as the source of power for streetcars, trains, and omnibuses. Trolleys—streetcars powered by an overhead electric line—were introduced in many cities. An important milestone in public transportation was the construction of subways to relieve the growing traffic congestion in urban areas. London opened the world's first subway line in 1863, and subway service began in Boston in 1897. Over time subways

Millions of people in urban areas around the world use public transportation every day. The Washington, D.C., metro opened in 1976.

New York Subways

In the early 1900s, New York City made plans to build a subway system to provide additional transportation for the growing population without adding to the city's bustling traffic. The first subway line, which ran along Broadway, opened in 1904. It was operated by the Interborough Rapid Transit Company, which extended the service to the Bronx the following year. By 1908 a tunnel under the East River made the construction of a line to Brooklyn possible. Subway service was later expanded to Queens.

transcontinental *extending across a continent*

subsidize *to assist with government funding*

facilities *something built or created to serve a particular function*

appeared in other major cities, and they became one of the most efficient forms of **mass transit**. Another type of public transportation, the cable car, was introduced in San Francisco in 1873 to take people up and down the city's steep hills.

During the 1900s motorized buses and improved rail systems transformed public transportation, replacing many of the systems in existence at the beginning of the century.

Public Transportation Today. Urban, regional, and long-distance transportation systems are an important element in modern society, moving people and goods along established routes to a variety of destinations. In the United States, buses carry most urban passenger traffic. Subways provide an important service in some places, and cities such as Sacramento and San Diego in California have constructed light rail systems—electric-powered urban train lines. In Europe, government support has led to a greater emphasis on light rail systems and subways, which Europeans prefer to buses because they cause less air pollution.

Public transportation plays an essential role in carrying commuters between city centers and outlying suburbs. Most commuter service is provided by trains. Buses, light rail systems, and ferries also serve commuters in some areas. Passenger service between cities is another part of public transportation. Airplanes, buses, and trains carry most of the intercity traffic. Amtrak trains, for example, connect a number of cities in the United States. Some intercity passengers travel by ferry.

Long-distance public transportation is provided by trains and airplanes. Before the mid-1900s almost all overseas trips were made by ship. Today, however, overseas passengers generally travel by plane. The United States, Canada, and Russia have **transcontinental** railways, but these systems carry fewer passengers than airlines.

Funding. Many public transportation systems receive government funding to supplement passenger fares. Mass transit systems are often heavily **subsidized** by the cities they serve. Many railway systems in Europe and elsewhere are government owned. American railroads are privately owned, except for the Amtrak passenger rail network, which has been partly funded by the government since its creation in 1970.

In the United States various transportation industries compete for limited federal and state funding. Some government funds go to **facilities,** networks, and services that are essential to transportation rather than to a particular industry. However, such funds may be very important to the well-being of an industry. Although bus and trucking companies receive no public funds directly, they benefit from the enormous amount of money that governments spend on highway, bridge, and tunnel construction and repair. By contrast, railroads generally pay for building and maintaining their own tracks.

Airports and waterways in the United States and elsewhere also receive government support. Projects such as the construction of new airports and improvements to older ones are often paid for by a combination of city, state, and federal funding. Government operation of air traffic control systems and construction of roads leading to airports assist the airlines in different ways. Ship and ferry lines benefit from the work of the U.S. Army Corps of Engineers, which builds and repairs dams, locks, and levees and dredges harbors and waterways.

Future of Public Transportation. Increasing concern over the impact of the automobile on traffic congestion and air pollution has contributed to a renewed interest in public transportation. Few U.S. cities can afford to build extensive new mass transit networks, but many are trying to update and expand earlier systems. These efforts include replacing older subway cars and buses, reserving specific highway lanes for bus traffic, and encouraging commuters to share rides in automobiles. Light rail systems, which are cheaper to build than subways, are increasingly popular.

Many countries are working to improve intercity transportation, especially rail networks. In Japan and several European countries, high-speed trains provide passenger service between major cities. In the United States, however, the development of similar high-speed trains has been slowed by the poor condition of many railroad tracks. However, Amtrak has begun to expand its high-speed service with the launch of its new Acela trains between Boston and Washington, D.C. *See also* AIRLINE INDUSTRY; AMTRAK; AUTOMOBILES, EFFECTS OF; BART (BAY AREA RAPID TRANSIT); BUSES; CABLE CARS AND FUNICULARS; COMMUTING; FERRIES; GOVERNMENT AND TRANSPORTATION; HIGH-SPEED TRAINS; LIGHT RAIL SYSTEMS; PASSENGERS; RAILROAD INDUSTRY; RAILWAY TRAINS, TYPES OF; SUBWAYS (METROS); TRANSPORTATION PLANNING; URBAN TRANSPORTATION.

Pullman Strike

injunction *court order to stop a particular action or to enforce a rule or regulation*

One of the most famous labor actions in U.S. history, the Pullman strike of 1894 temporarily shut down the nation's railroads and led to outbreaks of violence by railroad workers. President Grover Cleveland sent federal troops to restore order, and the government used an **injunction** to end the labor action. The strike and its outcome focused attention on the power of the federal government to take strong action against striking workers.

The Pullman strike involved the Pullman Palace Car Company, which manufactured railway sleeping cars. The action began after a financial slowdown hit the United States in 1893. To reduce costs during the business slump, the Pullman company cut wages to its workers by 25 percent. At the same time, however, it refused to lower the rents and other fees paid by workers living in the company-owned town near Chicago.

The workers' discontent created a windfall of new members for labor organizer Eugene V. Debs. By the spring of 1894 about 4,000 Pullman employees had joined his American Railway Union (ARU). On May 11, 1894, some 2,500 angry laborers in the Chicago area went on strike against the Pullman company. When company officials refused to negotiate with these workers, the ARU called on its members in other parts of the country to refuse to handle Pullman cars. This led to a general railroad strike. By late June the strike had spread throughout the nation, bringing railroads to a virtual standstill.

The strike caused a serious delay in the delivery of mail. As a result, U.S. Attorney General Richard Olney, a former lawyer for the railroads and bitter foe of organized labor, asked a federal court for an injunction

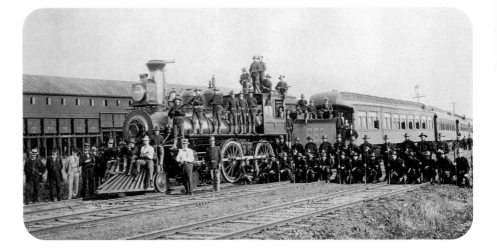

On May 11, 1894, some 2,500 angry railroad workers in the Chicago area went on strike against the Pullman Palace Car Company to protest a reduction in pay. By late June the strike had spread throughout the nation, bringing railroads to a virtual standstill. On July 4 President Cleveland ordered federal troops to Chicago to end the disorder.

against the strikers. The injunction ordered the workers to halt their interference with the transport of the mail and, more generally, with interstate commerce.

Striking workers ignored the court order, and an angry group in Chicago attacked a mail train. President Cleveland responded by sending 2,500 federal troops to Chicago on July 4. Mobs of strikers greeted the troops, and riots broke out. Rioting also occurred in other cities, causing much destruction to railroad property.

While the federal troops worked to end the disorder, Eugene Debs and other labor leaders were arrested (and later convicted) for violating the injunction. By July 20 the strike was over, the trains were running again, and the federal troops had been recalled.

In 1895 the U.S. Supreme Court upheld the use of a court injunction in the Pullman strike. The decision gave industry a powerful weapon against organized labor. It also convinced many workers that the government could not be trusted to play a neutral role in disputes between labor and management. *See also* LABOR UNIONS; RAILROADS, HISTORY OF; RAILROAD WORKERS.

Race Cars

Cars used in auto racing are designed for speed and sometimes for endurance. They include a variety of types, from vehicles built specifically for the sport to ordinary passenger cars that have been modified to boost their speed and power. The five basic types—high-performance cars, stock cars, sports cars, drag-racing cars, and land speed record cars—compete in different kinds of races.

High-performance cars are extremely expensive vehicles designed to reach speeds of more than 200 miles (320 km) per hour. Spoilers, winglike structures attached to the front and rear ends of the racing car, are the most distinctive feature. Air passes over the spoilers, creating downward pressure on the vehicle and providing the traction necessary to make turns at high speeds. Many specially built racing cars have a shell made of a strong, lightweight material such as aluminum or carbon fiber, a rear engine, an open cockpit, and wide racing tires. Formula One, or Grand Prix, cars are the most costly cars because each one is custom designed and built to order. Indy cars, which race in the famous

Cars used in auto racing are designed for speed and endurance. Formula One cars, such as the one in this photo, are the most expensive race cars because each one is custom designed and built-to-order.

Indianapolis 500, are similar to Formula One cars that burn methanol—a type of alcohol.

In the United States, the most popular form of automobile racing involves stock cars. These resemble late-model American cars in most respects but are significantly more powerful. Although much heavier than other race cars, they can reach speeds of 200 miles (320 km) per hour. Stock cars are used in the Winston Cup series of races, which includes the Daytona 500 in Daytona Beach, Florida.

Sports cars form another category of racers. Production sports cars have the same shape as their factory-built counterparts, but they are assembled on a special racing framework. Endurance cars, such as those used in the 24-hour race in Le Mans, France, may have turbo-charged engines. Specially built sports racing cars feature rear engines, rear spoilers, and enclosed cockpits.

Designed for rapid acceleration, drag-racing cars can go from a standing start to speeds of more than 290 miles (467 km) per hour in as little as five seconds. They compete on a quarter-mile (0.4-km) track. Most of the fastest dragsters have a rear-mounted engine and large rear tires. The car itself is not much more than a long, narrow frame with a single-seat cockpit for the driver with small, thin front tires that offer the least amount of **drag**.
See also AUTOMOBILES; AUTOMOBILES, PARTS OF.

drag slowing effect of an opposing force, such as friction, on a vehicle

Radar

Radar is an electronic device widely used by the military and in civilian transportation. Short for "radio detecting and ranging," radar can detect objects many miles away and determine their distance, direction, and speed. Radar works in daylight, at night, and in fog, rain, or other weather conditions that usually make it difficult for people to see objects at a distance.

sonar *short for sound navigation and ranging; system that uses sound waves to locate underwater objects*

Radar is based on scientific principles first discovered in the mid-1800s. Experiments in the early 1900s led to the development of radar equipment, and efforts to improve technology increased in the 1930s. Radar was first put to practical use during World War II as a way to track planes and warn of aerial bombing raids. At the same time ships began using a similar technology based on sound, known as **sonar,** to detect enemy submarines. Scientists continued to improve radar after the war, making it more accurate and sensitive.

Radar Systems.
There are several types of radar systems. Most have four main parts: a transmitter, an antenna, a receiver, and an indicator or display. In pulse radar—the most common type of radar system—the transmitter produces very short pulses of radio waves, or microwaves. These pulses, usually about 200 to 300 per second, are sent out in a narrow beam by the antenna. When the beam strikes an object, some of the pulses bounce backward. Called echoes, these reflected pulses are picked up by the antenna and sent to the receiver, which increases their strength. They then go to the indicator or display, where the radar operator receives information about the object.

Many radar systems use a rotating antenna and a circular display called a plan position indicator (PPI). The center of the PPI screen represents the location of the antenna. Its outer edge is the maximum range of the radar, which may be hundreds of miles or more. The echoes picked up by the antenna appear on the PPI as bright spots called blips. A radar operator can determine the distance and direction of objects by observing the position and movement of the blips on the display.

Doppler radar is most effective for determining the speed of moving objects. Instead of sending out pulses, Doppler radar transmits a continuous beam of microwaves at a set frequency. When this beam strikes a moving object, the reflected echoes will be at a higher or lower frequency depending on whether the object is approaching or moving away. The receiver automatically calculates the distance and speed of the object based on the changed frequency. The radar speed detectors used by police and some weather radar equipment are based on Doppler radar.

Uses of Radar.
Radar serves a wide variety of functions in transportation. It plays a vital role in aviation in such basic areas as directing the flow of air traffic, monitoring the positions and altitudes of aircraft, and helping planes land when runways are obscured by fog. Aboard ships, radar is used to detect the presence of nearby vessels, shorelines, and other hazards. The military relies on radar in missile defense, for tracking satellites, and in intelligence gathering.

Radar has an important role in weather observation and forecasting, including locating and tracking storms. In addition, scientists use radar to follow the migrations of birds, to map the surface of the Earth, to measure and chart ocean currents, to investigate the upper atmosphere, and to study the Moon and other planets. Finally, the police depend on radar to catch speeding drivers. *See also* AIRPORTS; AIR TRAFFIC CONTROL; LORAN; NAVIGATION; SONAR.

Rafts

maneuver *to make a series of changes in course*

A raft is a square or rectangular platform used for carrying people and goods on waterways. One of the earliest and most basic forms of watercraft, rafts are constructed from lightweight materials such as logs or reeds that are held together with wooden pegs, vines, ropes, or twisted strips of animal skin. Poles, paddles, or sails may be used to **maneuver** a raft.

For thousands of years, people living by the Tigris and Euphrates Rivers in the Middle East traveled downstream on rafts. Made of timber platforms, their craft floated on inflated goatskins. Ancient Egyptians made rafts by tying together bundles of reeds, and drawings on Egyptian pottery from 3000 B.C. show rafts with sails. Historians believe that Polynesian islanders used rafts to travel thousands of miles across the Pacific Ocean and settle Hawaii around A.D. 800. In 1947 Norwegian explorer Thor Heyerdahl demonstrated that large rafts could indeed make such a voyage. He and five companions constructed a balsa-wood raft named *Kon-Tiki* and sailed it more than 4,300 miles (6,920 km) across the Pacific Ocean from Peru to eastern Polynesia.

Rafts played an important part in the development of early seaports. People who lived inland loaded their cargo onto rafts that drifted with the current down the river. When the goods arrived at the mouth of the river, they would be transferred to a boat and shipped out to sea. During the 1800s Americans used flatboats, or large rafts, for commerce and passenger transportation on the Ohio and Mississippi Rivers.

Although larger and more powerful craft have generally replaced rafts in the modern world, they are still found in some regions. For example, the *jangada,* a lightweight balsa-wood raft, is valued by fishermen along Brazil's northeastern coast, and Peruvians lash bundles of reeds together to form a *caballito.* The Taiwanese construct seaworthy rafts from long, curved bamboo poles. *See also* BARGES; FLATBOATS; HEYERDAHL, THOR.

Railroad Barons

manipulate *to manage or influence in a clever or dishonest way*

Between the end of the Civil War in 1865 and the beginning of World War I in 1914, railroads were the fastest-growing business in the United States. A handful of financiers gained control of a large part of the industry and made enormous fortunes by building new lines or buying up existing ones. These extremely powerful and wealthy individuals came to be known as railroad barons, or robber barons. Although they were scorned for their greed and ruthlessness, a few of these financiers managed their railroads with skill and dedication.

One of the most notorious of the barons was Cornelius Vanderbilt (1794–1877), who worked his way from poverty to a reported worth of more than $100 million at the time of his death. After a long career in the shipping industry, he bought his first railroad in 1863. Vanderbilt soon built a railway empire between New York City and Chicago and was the moving force behind the construction of the Grand Central railroad station in New York City. He acquired much of his wealth by **manipulating** his own company's stocks, but such business practices were neither unusual nor unacceptable at the time.

Jay Gould was one of the "railroad barons" who controlled the U.S. railroad industry in the mid-1800s.

transcontinental *extending across a continent*

Vanderbilt's leading competitor in the East was Jay Gould (1836–1892). Gould became director of the Erie Railroad in 1867 and soon began to manipulate the company's stocks. When Vanderbilt attempted to seize control of the Erie line to expand his influence in the region, Gould defeated his rival's plans. In 1873 he turned his attention to the West, where the federal government was making land grants to companies that would build railroad tracks. Gould invested in numerous regional lines in the West, eventually owning or controlling the Denver Pacific, Kansas Pacific, Missouri Pacific, and Union Pacific Railroads. He accumulated a fortune, but his rail lines had a reputation for poor service, lack of maintenance, and outdated technology.

Collis P. Huntington (1821–1900) also took advantage of opportunities in the West. In 1862 he won a federal grant for his company to build the Central Pacific Railroad, the western link in the first **transcontinental** rail line. Huntington and his associates made enormous profits from this line.

J. P. Morgan (1837–1913), one of the world's leading bankers and a founder of the United States Steel Corporation, entered the railroad industry in 1885. By merging several major lines in the East, he gained great power in New York, Pennsylvania, and Ohio. Morgan became involved in reforming railway companies, and in the process he gained control of much of their stock.

Out west James J. Hill (1838–1916) represented a new generation of railroad barons—still rich, still tough, but filled with a genuine understanding of railroads and a passionate vision of their role in America's growth. Known as the "empire builder," Hill extended the nation's railway system into the Pacific Northwest and controlled the Great Northern group of railroad companies.

In 1898 Edward H. Harriman (1848–1909) gained control of the Union Pacific line and used his effective management skills to rescue it from ruin. He later acquired the Southern Pacific Railroad, and at the beginning of the 1900s owned more lines than any other American would ever own.

The railroad barons charged high freight rates and discouraged competition. By the early 1900s, many Americans were clamoring for a reform of the railway system. Unrest and labor strikes, together with the introduction of the automobile, would soon check the power of the railroad barons. *See also* Railroad Industry; Railroads, History of.

Railroad Industry

The railroad industry plays a vital role in the economies of the United States and other nations. Each day trains carry many thousands of passengers and tons of freight. The world's rail systems—ranging from lumbering freight trains to the most technologically advanced high-speed trains—travel over more than 750,000 miles (1,206,750 km) of track.

In the United States, the main business of railroads is in moving cargo. Passenger traffic plays a much smaller role in the industry than it did in the 1800s. However, in Europe, Japan, and other parts of the world, transporting people as well as goods remains an important function of railroads.

Major Railroad Lines

Almost every country in the world has at least one railroad; some have many. Both private companies and public agencies operate railroads. In the United States, almost all railroad companies are privately owned. In Europe and other world regions, by contrast, the major rail companies are under government control.

The United States. About 500 railroad companies, ranging from small tourist railroads to large freight lines, operate in the United States. Amtrak, the largest passenger railroad in the nation, is run by the National Railroad Passenger Corporation, an agency created and partly funded by the government. The Alaska Railroad, controlled by the state of Alaska, is one of the few other publicly owned lines.

The largest U.S. railroad companies are all freight lines. Among the best-known names in the industry are Burlington Northern Santa Fe, the Union Pacific Railroad, CSX Corporation, and Norfolk Southern Corporation. Burlington Northern and Union Pacific operate in the Midwest and the West, and CSX and Norfolk Southern serve the eastern half of the country.

Worldwide. In other parts of the world, railroads are generally owned and operated by national governments. The majority of Canadian passenger trains are run by the publicly funded VIA Rail Canada. The Canadian National Railroad and CP Rail, however, are privately owned.

The most modern and advanced passenger railroad lines in the world are in Europe and Japan. The French TGV trains, the fastest passenger trains in the world, travel at speeds up to 186 miles per hour (299 km per hour). The Shinkansen high-speed trains in Japan carry passengers between Tokyo and stations to the north and west. European and Japanese railroads operate with government funding because they are considered vital elements of the economy and society.

Russia, India, China, and South Africa all have extensive rail networks. The Russian system, with about 95,630 miles (153,870 km) of track, is one of the world's largest. In India, the first country in Asia to build a railway, train service has expanded to include about 66,970 miles (107,755 km) of routes.

Many of the railroad systems in Latin America, Africa, and various parts of Asia were originally built by Europeans during the colonial period. Now run by the individual countries, they are not yet as efficient or reliable as the trains in Europe, Japan, and the United States.

Construction and Maintenance

Most railroad construction took place in the 1800s and early 1900s, when companies around the world laid hundreds of thousands of miles of track and created vast railway networks linking cities and regions. Since that time some new railways have been created, but most

Classifying Trains

The U.S. government classifies railroads in different ways. One system divides railroads into line-haul companies and switching and terminal companies. Line-haul companies are railroads that own and operate major rail lines. Switching and terminal companies own facilities such as the tracks and equipment around major railroad terminals. Another widely used system of classification is based on income. Class I railroads are companies that earn more than $250 million per year. Class II railroads earn between $20 million and $250 million, and Class III railroads earn less than $20 million.

Between 1830 and 1916, railroad workers laid more than 250,000 miles (402,250 Km) of track in the United States. Since that time, most construction work has involved improving and maintaining existing tracks, bridges, tunnels, and railroad yards. In this photo, railroad workers repair sections of track along the Burlington Northern line in Wyoming.

construction work now involves improving and maintaining existing tracks, bridges, tunnels, and railroad yards.

Roadbeds and Tracks. Railroad tracks are laid on a specially prepared surface called a roadbed, which acts as a foundation for the track. The roadbed is generally made of gravel or crushed stones that have been graded, or pressed down to create a smooth and level surface.

The railroad track itself consists of two parallel steel rails, usually 39 feet (about 12 m) long, fastened by metal spikes and steel tie plates to wooden beams called crossties. Gravel and stones from the roadbed hold the crossties in place and provide good drainage for the track.

The distance between the two rails, called the gauge, must be the same at all points so that trains remain firmly on the track. Each country has a standard gauge for its railway lines. This allows railroad cars, which have uniform spacing between their wheels, to travel over the entire rail network. The standard gauge in the United States, Canada, Mexico, and most of Europe is 4 feet 8½ inches (about 1.44 m).

Many railway lines are built with two or more tracks laid side by side. This enables trains to travel in opposite directions at the same time. Lines with only a single track have sidings, short lengths of track that branch off from the main track. When two trains traveling in opposite directions approach each other, one goes onto the siding and waits until the other train passes.

To maintain tracks, railroads must replace old rails and crossties that have become worn or damaged. In the 1800s railway lines were laid by hand. Today, however, much of the work is done by machines. Most European countries have kept their railroad tracks in excellent condition. In the United States some tracks are equal to the best in Europe, but others are old and in need of repair.

Bridges and Tunnels. Trains have difficulty climbing steep inclines. For this reason, railroads try to lay tracks on as level a surface as possible. In some places this can be done simply by filling in low spots, cutting into small hills, adjusting the height of the roadbed, and curving the tracks to circle around mountains. In other places, however, railroad engineers need to build bridges and tunnels to cross deep valleys and pass through mountain barriers. Tunnels and bridges also enable railroad lines to pass under or over rivers and other bodies of water. Railroad bridges and tunnels require regular maintenance and repair to keep them safe.

Railway Yards. Freight trains begin and end their runs in classification yards, areas of railroad terminals where trains are organized for departure. Classification yards have many sets of tracks connected by switches. Each track splits up into various sidings, like the branches of a tree. All the railroad cars going to a particular destination are assigned to a specific siding. Arriving trains enter the yard on a main track at one end; departing trains exit along a track at the other end.

There are two types of classification yards: flat yards and hump yards. In flat yards, the cars from incoming trains are moved to the proper sidings by locomotives called switch engines. These engines travel back and forth between sidings many times, and the yard workers use hand-operated switching devices to guide them. Arranging railroad cars by this method can be a slow process.

Hump yards are much more efficient. When a train arrives, the locomotive is uncoupled and a switching engine pushes the cars to the top of a low hill—the hump. As the cars roll down the opposite side of the hump, an operator in a control tower switches each one onto its assigned track or siding. Special braking devices help control the speed of the rolling cars. Most modern hump yards are heavily automated, with computers handling many operations.

Consolidation and Mergers

Railroads have always been expensive to operate. Over the years, the high costs have forced some companies out of business. Others have joined together in an attempt to operate more efficiently and profitably.

Maintenance work, storage of cars, and repairs are usually done at the train yard.

merger combining two or more organizations

consolidation unification of different elements

Romance of the Rails

In the past certain famous passenger trains known for luxury and speed contributed to a romantic image of railroad travel. In the United States, the sleek Twentieth Century Limited ran between New York City and Chicago, and the California Zephyr followed a scenic route, crossing the Rocky Mountains on its journey between Chicago and San Francisco. The Orient Express offered luxury service and a hint of international intrigue—mostly because of movies—on its route between Paris and Constantinople (now Istanbul), Turkey. Some famous trains such as the California Zephyr still operate. The Trans-Siberian Express crosses the width of Russia from Moscow to Vladivostok, providing the longest train ride in the world.

monopoly control of a market or product by a single company or country

In the late 1800s, the United States had many railroad companies, but competition and financial troubles led a number of small railroads to merge with larger ones. By 1906 nearly two-thirds of all the railway lines in the nation were controlled by just seven major companies.

After World War I, the U.S. Congress passed legislation that encouraged further **mergers** as a way of improving railroad efficiency. The resulting **consolidation** of companies helped make the railroads fairly profitable in the 1920s. However, competition from new forms of transportation, such as automobiles and pipelines, soon began to challenge the dominance of railroads.

During the Great Depression of the 1930s, many railroad companies suffered severe financial problems and were forced out of business. The industry recovered during World War II by carrying a record volume of passengers and freight. After the war, however, the increasing use of motor vehicles and airplanes caused a sharp decline in business, especially in passenger service.

Eventually the federal government stepped in to help the troubled railroads. In 1970 Congress created Amtrak, a passenger railroad formed by combining a number of existing companies. A few years later, it merged several bankrupt northeastern freight railroads into Conrail (Consolidated Rail Corporation), which later became quite profitable.

Mergers between railroads continued to take place into the 1990s. In 1995, for example, Burlington Northern merged with the Santa Fe Railroad; the following year, Union Pacific combined with Southern Pacific. In 1999, CSX and Norfolk Southern took over Conrail and divided its routes, which they added to their own railway systems.

Competition

In the 1930s the railroad industry lost the near **monopoly** it had enjoyed on much of the land-based freight and passenger transportation in the United States. Cars, trucks, buses, pipelines, and airplanes provided alternate means of moving people and goods.

Most Americans have abandoned railroad travel for automobiles because of their flexibility or for airplanes because of their speed. Buses have also taken passengers away from railroads, especially in commuter and intercity service.

The railroads have lost freight-hauling business to other forms of transportation as well. Much of the competition in this area comes from the trucking industry. Airlines have also taken over certain types of cargo, including mail, that used to be carried by trains. Pipelines, which can transport liquids such as petroleum products easily and efficiently, provide freight competition too.

In the 1920s railroads carried about 75 percent of all freight moved between cities in the United States. Today they carry less than 40 percent. Meanwhile, intercity passenger service decreased from about 47 percent of passenger traffic in 1950 to less than 1 percent today. *See also* Amtrak; Baltimore and Ohio Railroad; Canadian Pacific Railway; Commuting; Conrail; Eurail System; Freight; Freight Trains; Government and Transportation; Light Rail Systems; Passengers;

Railroad Safety

The speed and power of railroads have always made them objects of danger as well as symbols of adventure and romance. Various systems have been developed to make railroads safer, from early manual methods of signaling to modern traffic control based on advanced computer technology.

Signaling and Traffic Control. Since the start of railroading, different trains have shared track, in some cases even traveling in opposite directions on the same track. To avoid collisions, some sort of signaling and traffic control system was needed.

In the early days these systems were rather crude. One way trains avoided accidents was for engine crews to simply watch for the smoke of oncoming locomotives and then stop their own train. This method was far from foolproof, and as train speeds increased it did not allow engineers enough time to prevent collisions with oncoming trains. Train crews really needed to know well in advance what obstacles or track conditions lay ahead.

As track mileage grew in the mid-1800s, so did the number of accidents. Railroads looked for ways to improve traffic control. Their efforts included having a station master climb a pole to watch for trains and descend to ring a bell when he saw one approaching. Railroads also set up poles halfway between stations, and any train that reached the pole first had the right-of-way. In other cases, an engineer was handed a colored stick upon arriving at a station, giving his train the right-of-way to the next station.

Railroads also tried various methods of signaling. Flags and lights were hung on trains to indicate the start and end of a train and how many cars it was pulling. By the 1840s railroads used semaphore signaling, which involved movable arms mounted on a post. Different positions of the arms meant "proceed," "proceed with caution," or "stop." Signaling and traffic control systems were tied together in the 1850s by the telegraph, which enabled railroads to pass traffic information quickly from station to station. At the end of the 1800s semaphore signals were replaced by colored lights similar to the motor vehicle traffic signals of today.

The Block System. An important advance in railroad traffic control occurred in the 1860s with the development of the block system, a method of controlling the positions of trains on a single track.

The speed and weight of trains make it difficult for them to stop quickly. For this reason, it is very important to have adequate space between trains traveling on the same track. At first this was accomplished by scheduling, with trains leaving railway stations at intervals that would ensure enough space between them. This system of scheduling had drawbacks, however. If a train was stopped or delayed, it had to be

Since the start of railroading, signaling systems have been necessary to avoid collisions between trains. Gates, flashing lights, and bells are used at railroad crossings to indicate that a train is coming.

able to communicate its position before the train behind got too close to stop. The block system solved this problem.

In the block system, railroad track was divided into lengths called blocks, with each block from 1 to 2 miles (1.6 to 3.2 km) long. Only one train was allowed in each block at a time, and signals indicated when a train could enter or leave a block. For many years, railroad workers controlled the blocks manually, throwing switches to change the signals. In 1872 automatic block signals were introduced. They work through an electric current that runs through the rails. When trains enter and leave blocks of track, their wheels automatically trigger signals to stop or proceed.

Modern railroads still use the block system of traffic control, although many are now adopting a moving block system in which the blocks are not a fixed distance on the track. Instead communications devices on trains send signals through the track, and the signals are picked up and processed by computers on other trains on the same track. The computers automatically adjust the speed of the trains to maintain a safe distance between them.

Centralized Traffic Control.
Introduced in the 1920s, a computerized system known as centralized traffic control (CTC) revolutionized the management of rail traffic. CTC allows railroads to control traffic along several hundred miles of tracks from a central location instead of from different stations along routes.

CTC uses automatic block signals for trains following one another on the same track. All other switches and signals are controlled from a central location. Operators at the CTC center can watch the movement of every train in the rail system on electronic diagrams and direct traffic by using computers to set switches and signals. Because CTC can control large portions of a rail network with great efficiency, it has allowed railroads to eliminate many sections of multiple track.

Other Safety Systems and Features.
Modern trains rely on various other methods to ensure safety. A system known as automatic train protection (ATP) uses devices in the track to transmit warning signals to trains. First developed in the 1920s, ATP can send instructions to speed up, slow down, or stop. If an engineer ignores the signals, the ATP system will take over and automatically control the train. ATP is most widely used on urban commuter and mass transit trains.

Special care must be taken at grade-level crossings—locations where railroad tracks cross a roadway—to prevent collisions between trains and pedestrians or vehicles. Gates, flashing lights, and bells are often used to indicate that a train is coming. In the 1990s the U.S. Department of Transportation began a program of eliminating large numbers of grade-level crossings and improving warning systems at the remaining ones to reduce the risk of accidents.

Other railroad safety features include electronic devices that can detect damaged wheels on railroad cars and equipment dragging on the track and warn train crews of these problems. The use of vestibules, flexible covered passageways between passenger cars, helps protect passengers

What Price Safety?

The 1880s saw the invention of two important railroad safety devices, the air brake and the automatic coupler. Air brakes were much more effective than the hand brakes used at the time, even for long trains moving downhill. The automatic coupler avoided many disfiguring accidents among railway workers caused by the manual coupling of railroad cars.

However, air brakes and automatic couplers were expensive items at a time when labor was cheap, and railroad officials resisted using them. A federal law passed in 1893 required all trains to be equipped with the two devices. The result was a 60 percent reduction in the accident rate among railway workers.

walking between cars on a moving train. Railroads also promote safety by keeping railroad bridges and tunnels in good repair.

In the early years of railroading, train accidents were quite common, sometimes resulting in several hundred deaths each year. As a result of efforts to improve railroad safety, the rate of accidents and deaths on railroads has declined dramatically since the 1800s. *See also* ACCIDENTS; COMMUNICATION SYSTEMS; RAILROAD INDUSTRY; RAILROADS, HISTORY OF; REGULATION OF TRANSPORTATION; SIGNALING.

Railroads, History of

The development of railroads in the early 1800s revolutionized overland transportation. Railroads offered a fast, reliable, and relatively inexpensive way to move people and goods over long distances. Compared with the horse-drawn wagons and stagecoaches that crept over rough country roads at only a few miles per hour, even the earliest trains seemed quick. Moreover, they could carry much more cargo.

The railroads had a major impact on the economies and societies of the countries that built them. They helped expand trade. Manufacturers, farmers, and merchants could ship goods over long distances, reaching larger markets and increasing sales. They made traveling for business and pleasure easier, safer, and more enjoyable. As a result, people began to move around more, reducing regional differences as individuals from different areas came into contact more frequently. In addition, building and running the railroads created tens of thousands of jobs, providing a boost for national economies.

Railroads helped open up new areas for settlement, mining, and other uses of natural resources. In the United States, trains carried thousands of people to the western states each year during the 1800s, expanding cities and settling the frontier. At the same time, the railroads brought back cattle, metal ores, and other goods from the West to markets in the East.

The heyday of the railroads lasted only until the early 1900s, when new forms of transportation—automobiles, trucks, and later, airplanes—began competing for the business of carrying people and cargo. As the volume of their freight and passenger traffic declined, railroads were forced to merge, modernize, and streamline their operations just to survive.

The Development of Railroads Worldwide

Railroad history began in Europe in the 1500s, when miners pushed wooden carts along wooden rails to haul coal out of mines. A century later, these primitive railroads had been extended well beyond the openings of mines, and horses pulled the carts to the nearest waterway, where the coal could be loaded on barges or ships.

Rails. The early railroads ran over wooden rails, which wore away with the movement of the carts. In 1776, metal plates were placed on top of the wooden rails to protect them from wear. English inventor

William Jessop introduced cast iron rails in 1789. Next came wrought iron rails and then steel rails after the mid-1800s.

Steel rails lasted for years, even in places where the old iron rails had worn out in a matter of months. Meanwhile, in 1830 American inventor Robert Stevens designed a rail shaped like an upside-down T, with projecting rims called flanges. Early iron rails also had a flange to carry carts with ordinary wheels. But by the late 1700s the flanges had been eliminated and the wheels of railroad carts had flanges instead. Stevens's T-shaped rail became the standard shape for rails. Stevens also introduced the use of wooden crossties, set in gravel beneath the rails to form the roadbed for railroad track.

Further Information
To learn more about the railroad industry; rail workers, unions, and strikes; government regulation; and specific railroads, see the related articles listed at the end of this entry.

Steam Locomotives. A crucial factor in the history of railroads was the development of steam power to replace horse power. In the late 1700s English inventor Richard Trevithick designed a steam engine that he mounted on a carriage that could travel on rails. The vehicle became the world's first successful steam locomotive in 1804, when Trevithick used it to pull five wagons about 9 miles (14 km). Others worked to improve the steam locomotive.

In 1814 British inventor George Stephenson constructed the first steam engine that could outrun a horse team while pulling a load. Stephenson went on to construct the first public steam-powered railroad in 1825, the Stockton and Darlington Railway, a 12-mile (19-km) freight line in Britain. (Horse-powered public railways had been operating there since 1803.)

Stephenson made other important contributions to railroading. In 1829 he developed the Rocket, a reliable steam locomotive with a top speed of 36 miles (58 km) per hour. He also introduced the idea of standard gauge—the distance between the two rails—and set it at 4 feet 8½ inches (1.44 m). This gauge was adopted by railroads in many countries, including the United States. In addition, Stephenson built the Liverpool and Manchester Railway, which in 1830 became the first steam railway to offer regular passenger service.

Railroads Around the World. These early developments stimulated a railroad construction boom in many countries. More than 400 railroads were built in Britain during the 1840s, and by 1860 the country had a total of 8,000 miles (12,872 km) of track. The first railroad in the United States went into service in 1830, and Canada's first line began operation six years later.

The earliest German railroad started running in 1835. Although France opened its first rail line in 1828, construction of additional lines proceeded slowly. Other countries in western Europe began building railroads in the 1840s and 1850s. But within 20 to 30 years, each had several thousand miles of track.

Eastern European nations opened rail lines somewhat later, in the 1860s. Russia's first railway began service in 1837, but expansion went slowly. By 1860 only 600 miles (965 km) of track had been laid, and work on the Trans-Siberian Railroad did not begin until 1891. Finally completed in 1916, the Trans-Siberian line stretched 5,787 miles (9,311 km) across Russia, making it the longest single line in the world.

In 1814 British engineer George Stephenson built the first steam engine that could outrun a horse team while pulling a load. Here, two men drive one of the steam locomotives invented by Stephenson in the 1820s.

Outside Europe and the United States, railroad construction got under way later. Although the first rail systems in Central and South America opened in the 1850s, some countries in the region did not build railroads until the 1870s and 1880s. The first railroads in Asia and Africa were built by the British in the 1850s. Japan opened a railway in 1872 and China in the early 1880s. Most nations possessed railroads by the late 1800s.

Governments soon realized the importance of railroads to their economies, communications, and national defense. Many responded by taking control of privately owned lines. Except for the United States and Canada, most countries today have rail systems controlled fully or in part by the national government.

Development of the Modern Railroad. During the period of great railroad construction in the 1800s, engineers were constantly working to make railroads better—safer, more comfortable, and faster. Advances in safety included new signaling systems introduced in the mid-1800s as well as the automatic car coupler and compressed air brakes, invented by the American George Westinghouse in the late 1800s.

Railroad passenger cars—at first little more than stagecoaches with special wheels—were enclosed and made more comfortable. American railroads introduced Pullman sleeping cars and dining cars in the 1860s. Specialized freight cars, such as tankers for hauling oil, also appeared about this time. Railway cars had been made largely of wood, but in the late 1800s, steel cars began to replace the wooden ones.

At the same time steam locomotives became larger and more powerful. Some were giants weighing several hundred tons and delivering up to 7,000-horsepower. By the 1870s electric locomotives had come into

Advances in technology prompted the development of large and powerful locomotives, such as the one shown here. Some weighed several hundred tons and delivered up to 7,000-horsepower.

pollutant *something that contaminates the environment*

use, and diesel locomotives were introduced in 1913. Electric and diesel locomotives required fewer people to operate, were more efficient, and gave off fewer **pollutants** than steam locomotives. Diesels also delivered greater power. As a result, electric and diesel engines have replaced steam on nearly all the world's rail lines, bringing a close to the age of steam.

Railroads in the United States

Railroads played a crucial role in the history of the United States. They linked distant regions and helped unify the nation as it developed and expanded along with the railroads. The vast size of the country required a huge rail network. By the early 1900s, more than 250,000 miles (402,250 km) of track had been laid—at the time, the largest rail system in the world.

Early Railroads. In the early 1800s, a few horse-powered railroads were introduced in the United States. As in Europe, they featured wooden rails and horse-drawn carts. Then, in 1825, inventor John Stevens built an experimental "steam wagon," which he demonstrated on a circular track at his home in Hoboken, New Jersey. Stevens's vehicle was the first railroad locomotive in the Americas.

Five years later Tom Thumb, a small steam locomotive built by Peter Cooper of New York, made a trial run on a 13-mile (21-km) section of Baltimore and Ohio Railroad track. The Tom Thumb proved too small for regular use. Later that year, on December 25, 1830, the South Carolina Canal and Railroad Company launched the first scheduled, steam-powered railway service in the United States with a locomotive called Best Friend of Charleston.

During the next five years, new railroads sprang up in a number of states, and workers laid more than 1,000 miles (1,609 km) of track. For the most part, rail lines radiated outward from ports such as New York, Philadelphia, Baltimore, and Charleston, connecting these eastern cities with markets in rural areas. During these early years, the novelty of railroad travel lured many passengers, and trains carried more people than freight.

By 1850 the nation had about 9,000 miles (14,480 km) of track, and railroads had become accepted as a useful form of transportation. Shipping goods by rail was generally much faster and more reliable than by horse and wagon or by boat. Railroad rates may have been higher than those of water transport, but they were much cheaper than the rates of freight companies using horses.

By this time the typical American locomotive had been developed. Its front four wheels were mounted together in a unit called a leading truck, which was designed to handle a curving route. The truck could swivel slightly as the locomotive rounded a bend. Behind the truck were four driving wheels, which actually moved the train.

American steam locomotives in the mid-1800s burned wood for fuel and were painted in bright colors. Other typical features of these locomotives included a bell, a whistle, and a cowcatcher. This last item was necessary because early American railroads rarely fenced off their tracks from the surrounding land, and livestock often wandered onto rail lines with unfortunate results.

A railroad-building boom in the 1850s boosted the total track mileage in the United States from 9,000 to 30,000 miles (14,480 to 48,270 km). Every state east of the Mississippi River could be reached by rail, and Chicago became a transportation center with 11 different rail lines leading to it. Thanks to the railroads, the population of Chicago increased dramatically during the decade.

Land Grants.   In 1850 the federal government set up a land grant program that contributed to the rapid growth of railroads and the settlement of the nation's frontier. Under the program, the federal government gave land—which included a strip of land for the rail lines as well as adjoining acreage—to the states. The states, in turn, transferred the property to railroad companies. These companies sold off the adjoining lands to help pay for building the rail lines. In return for the land grants, the railroads were required to carry U.S. mail at a reduced rate and to transport federal troops and supplies at half the normal cost.

The land grant program eventually turned over to the railroads about 130 million acres (52,650,000 hectares) of public land. The investment proved worthwhile. The new rail lines stimulated economic growth, provided jobs for thousands of workers, and helped draw millions of new settlers to the West.

The Civil War.   By 1860, just before the Civil War, railroads had become the dominant means of moving people and goods in the United States. They offered reliable and efficient transport in all types of

Setting the Time

Before the 1880s each community in the United States kept its own time, based on the position and movement of the Sun. As a result, nearby towns often ran on slightly different time. This caused tremendous confusion for railroads when they tried to set up schedules and timetables. To solve the problem, the railroads divided the nation into four time zones and set a single, standard time for each zone. Communities around the nation soon adopted these standard times, making it easier to plan travel and other activities. The time zones became official in 1918, when the federal government established the first daylight saving time.

weather and moved large quantities of goods faster and more cheaply than any other transportation method.

The Civil War was the first armed conflict in which railroads played a major role. It showed how important railroads could be for moving troops rapidly and supplying large armies with war materials, food, and other necessities. During the war, both the Union and Confederate armies benefited from existing railroads. However, the rail system in the North was far more extensive than that of the South, and this became a factor in the northern victory.

Early in the war, the Confederates made good use of their railroads to move troops to battle. In the summer of 1861, thousands of Confederate soldiers were carried by rail from the Shenandoah Valley to Manassas, Virginia, where they won the Battle of Bull Run, the South's first major victory in the war. Later, in the autumn of 1863, the Union army shifted 25,000 soldiers from Washington, D.C., to Chattanooga, Tennessee, in one of the war's largest troop movements by rail. These soldiers helped break the Confederate siege of that city, a crucial victory for the North.

By the end of the Civil War, many rail lines in the United States had been damaged. The South suffered more destruction than the North. Despite the losses, the railroads had proven their usefulness, and efforts to rebuild led to a golden age of railroading.

The Golden Age. In the years after the Civil War, the railroads enjoyed unprecedented growth and came to dominate the transportation industry. A building boom created a network of rails reaching into virtually every corner of the nation. In the 1880s alone, railroads added 70,000 miles (112,630 km) of track. By 1916 the United States had reached a peak of 254,000 miles (408,686 km) of rail lines.

By 1850 the United States had about 9,000 miles (14,480 km) of track. A railroad-building boom in the 1850s boosted the track mileage to 30,000 miles (48,270 km); by 1916 there were 254,000 miles (408,686 km) of rail lines.

transcontinental *extending across a continent*

The Golden Spike

Construction on the first transcontinental railroad in the United States began in 1862 with crews working for the Union Pacific Railroad laying track westward from Omaha, Nebraska, while workers on the Central Pacific Railroad laid track eastward from Sacramento, California. It took thousands of laborers—many of them Chinese immigrants—six years to close the 1,775-mile (2,856-km) gap between the two cities. When the two rail lines finally met at Promontory Point, Utah, on May 10, 1869, railroad officials completed the job by driving the last spike themselves. To mark the historic occasion, they used specially made silver sledgehammers and pounded a golden spike into place.

consolidation *unification of different elements*

corruption *dishonesty or improper behavior*

One of the notable achievements of this period was the construction of the nation's first **transcontinental** rail line. Started in 1862, the line was completed in 1869. Eventually five cross-country lines were built, although shorter rail lines continued to spring up in the West and elsewhere in the nation.

The railroads contributed to the expansion of American industry in the late 1800s and benefited from it as well. By transporting goods across the country at reasonable rates, railroads enabled industries to sell products nationwide instead of just within a certain region. This expanded market played an important role in developing a national economy. Meanwhile, the amount of cargo moved by rail increased dramatically. By 1916 the railroads also carried 98 percent of all passenger traffic between cities.

As rail transport expanded, employment by railroads grew by leaps and bounds, soaring from 163,000 workers in 1865 to 1,700,000 in 1917. Many railroad workers joined labor unions, and their demands for higher wages and better working conditions sometimes resulted in violent clashes between workers and railroad owners, such as in the Pullman strike of 1894. Labor organizers eventually forced railroads to increase wages and improve working conditions.

At the end of the 1800s, a wave of **consolidation** swept through the railroad industry. Small and large railroads were bought up and combined into massive rail networks. By the early 1900s just seven giant railroad corporations—owned by wealthy tycoons such as the Vanderbilts, Edward Harriman, James Hill, and Jay Gould—controlled about two-thirds of all U.S. railroads.

Railroads and the Government. Despite the many good things about rail transportation, the railroads faced a great deal of opposition. Farmers and cattle ranchers, in particular, criticized railroad policies on freight charges and special treatment for certain customers. Dependent on the railroads for shipping crops and livestock to market, the farmers and ranchers complained about the high rates that cut into their income. They also disliked the weekly pricing changes and rate wars, in which rates became very cheap for a time only to bounce back to new highs.

Organized efforts to counter railroad pricing policies began as early as 1867, when thousands of farmers in the West formed the National Grange of the Patrons of Husbandry. Responding to complaints by Grange members, several Midwestern states passed "Granger" laws regulating freight pricing in the 1870s. After the U.S. Supreme Court ruled in 1886 that states could only control rates within their own borders, the federal government stepped in and created the Interstate Commerce Commission (ICC) in 1887. The ICC had the power to monitor and regulate railroad rates throughout the nation and to enforce federal guidelines concerning competition among railroads.

Corruption in railroad companies became a problem in the second half of the 1800s as well. Corrupt railroad construction companies often charged excessive fees, allowing company officials to gain millions in extra profits. In the Credit Mobilier Scandal of 1872, for example, some railroad officials had received an estimated $23 million in additional profits from the building of the Union Pacific section of the transcontinental

manipulate to manage or influence in a clever or dishonest way

railroad. Meanwhile, certain railroad owners engaged in corrupt practices, including schemes to **manipulate** the value of railroad stocks on the stock market.

During the early 1900s, the federal government responded to railroad corruption by strengthening the powers of the Interstate Commerce Commission, giving it authority to regulate railroad rates, outlawing various railroad policies, and generally increasing its control over the railroads. Such changes began to seriously challenge the long-time dominance of the railroads and led to new difficulties.

Trouble for the Railroads.

Increasing federal control over the railroads solved some problems but created others. Despite rising labor and other costs in the early 1900s, the ICC refused to allow railroads to increase their rates. With less money to pay for maintenance and new equipment, the railroads had trouble providing normal services.

These difficulties grew when the United States entered World War I in 1917, and the demand for railroad services increased. To ensure that military transportation needs would be met, the federal government took the unprecedented step of assuming control of the railroads. Government managers raised rates and increased the wages of railroad workers, but they failed to keep up with maintenance.

To make matters worse, the railroads began to face increasing competition at this time from other forms of transportation. The construction of new electric rail lines for intercity travel cut into passenger volume on the major railroads. So, too, did the arrival of automobiles, motorbuses, and later, airplanes. Meanwhile, trucks provided new and growing competition for freight business, and pipelines took business away for the transport of oil.

With their dominance in the transportation industry already broken by government regulation and the rise of new forms of transportation, the railroads suffered further declines in the 1930s during the Great Depression. By 1938 a number of railroads were in or near bankruptcy. A massive increase in rail traffic during World War II revitalized the industry in the 1940s, but the return of peacetime left railroads facing lingering problems.

Since World War II.

Efforts to increase the efficiency of rail service after World War II changed the way railroads operate. Intermodal transport—the combination of air, sea, and ground transportation—became an important part of the railway business. Railroads built special flatbed cars capable of carrying large containers taken directly from ships and trucks. They also spent millions of dollars updating and replacing worn-out equipment.

Even so, railroads continued struggling to survive. Despite changes and modernization, labor unions insisted on protecting unnecessary jobs such as that of the firemen on diesel locomotives. Efforts to keep these workers employed—called "featherbedding"—increased railroad operating costs. At the same time, high taxes and strict federal regulation of rates and other aspects of rail operations held down railroad income.

In the 1960s and 1970s, railroads responded to their financial problems with a series of **mergers** and by forming conglomerates—large

merger combining two or more organizations

corporations in which different types of businesses are combined. But the ailing railroads continued to decline, especially their passenger service. Finally, the government was forced to step in and take action to save the railroads from ruin.

subsidize to assist with government funding

In 1970 the federal government formed the National Railroad Passenger Corporation—known as Amtrak—to provide **subsidized** passenger service. It also allowed the railroads to eliminate their own passenger operations, which had been losing money for decades. In 1973 the government created Conrail to take over the freight service of several failing railways in the Northeast. Then, in 1980, Congress passed the Staggers Rail Act, which cut federal regulation of railroad rates, enabling railways to increase their profits. Although these actions helped the struggling industry, railroads still face a number of problems.

In Canada, passenger rail service is also provided by a government corporation. Created in 1978, VIA Rail Canada operates trains between major cities as well as to remote northern regions.

Future of Railways. Although railroads are expensive to operate and maintain, they still form an important part of transportation systems around the world. In Europe, railroads play a significant role in passenger transportation. In the United States, by contrast, railroads provide only a small percentage of passenger service.

For moving large volumes of freight, especially bulky materials such as coal and gravel, railroads are generally more efficient than other forms of transportation. They also occupy relatively little space compared to highway systems, putting less stress on the environment. Relative to cars and trucks, railroads are also more fuel efficient. Basic advantages such as these are likely to keep railroads operating well into the future. *See also* Amtrak; Conrail; Engines; Eurail System; Freight Trains; Government and Transportation; Intermodal Transport; Interstate Commerce Commission; Labor Unions; Light Rail Systems; Passengers; Pullman Strike; Railroad Barons; Railroad Industry; Railroad Safety; Railroad Workers; Railway Stations; Regulation of Transportation; Stephenson, George; Transcontinental Railroad; Trans-Siberian Railroad.

Railroad Workers

Railroad workers have played a significant role in the history of transportation in the United States, building the first network to span the continent and establishing some of the nation's first labor unions. Although the railroads had a huge labor force in the past, the number of people employed by American railroads dropped sharply during the twentieth century. From a high point of 2 million workers in 1920, railroad employment had come down to about 83,000 in the late 1990s. Among the causes of this massive reduction are advances in railroad technology, a decline in the passenger and freight traffic of railways, and company mergers.

In other countries, railroads have remained important as transportation providers and employers. Two of the major railways in Canada, Canadian National and Canadian Pacific, each employ more than 20,000 workers. Russia, India, Japan, Great Britain, France, and Germany also have extensive rail networks supported by large numbers of workers.

Types of Workers. Perhaps the most well-known railroad workers are the crews that operate trains. Train crews generally include engineers, conductors, and assistant conductors. The job of the engineer is to operate the locomotive, while the conductor supervises the overall operation of the train. The assistant conductor performs tasks such as adding and removing cars from a train.

In the days of steam locomotives, firemen tended the boiler that generated steam. Some modern trains have an assistant engineer, who helps the engineer and supervises safety procedures. In addition to train crews, modern railroads employ a variety of other workers ranging from station agents, computer specialists, planners, marketing personnel, and lawyers to maintenance workers, mechanics, electricians, and many others.

Railroad Unions. Among the best organized groups in American labor, railroad unions have been responsible for important gains by workers in all industries. In its early days railroading was an incredibly dangerous profession. Between 1866 and 1870, for example, some 70 percent of all railroad workers were killed on the job. The desire to protect the workers and to improve their working conditions led to the establishment of labor unions for railroad employees.

The first railroad union was formed during the Civil War by engineers of the Michigan Central Railroad, which had provoked fierce opposition by cutting salaries and firing people who protested bad working conditions. The union was a success, and it soon became clear that engineers would have more power in dealing with management if they stuck together. In the mid-1860s representatives of 12 major railroads founded the Brotherhood of Locomotive Engineers.

After the Civil War other railroad workers began to organize unions. In 1868 the Order of Railway Conductors was formed to seek higher pay, better working conditions, and greater job security for conductors. Despite opposition by railroad executives, the union was quite successful in gaining better wages, hours, and safety.

Railroad firemen founded the Brotherhood of Locomotive Firemen and Engineers in 1873. One of its early officers, Eugene V. Debs, became a leading figure in the American labor movement in the late 1800s and early 1900s. The Brotherhood of Railway Brakemen was formed in 1883. By the early 1900s it was one of the largest rail unions, including yardmen, conductors, baggage handlers, and even bus drivers as well as brakemen.

Railroad unions remain strong today. The Brotherhood of Locomotive Engineers still represents most train engineers and operates safety and education programs for its members. The United Transportation Union includes conductors and other railroad workers as well as bus and transit service employees in the United States and Canada. Other industry

The number of people employed by American railroads dropped sharply from 2 million workers in 1920 to about 83,000 in the 1990s.

workers, such as those who build and maintain the tracks, belong to different unions.

Strikes and Benefits. Rail workers have participated in many labor strikes over the years in attempts to gain higher pay and other benefits. In fact, the first real labor strike in the United States, staged in 1855, involved workers of the Boston and Thompson Railroad. The strike actually occurred ten years before the formation of the first railroad union.

The first major railroad strike took place in 1877, halting most trains in the East. Federal troops broke up the strike, but only after a great deal of violence, including a gun battle between troops and rail workers in Pittsburgh. A successful strike against the Great Northern Railway in 1893 was followed the next year by a strike against the Pullman Palace Car Company. The Pullman strike became one of the most famous labor actions in U.S. history.

The threat of strikes by railroad unions during World War I led to a number of labor improvements, including the adoption of a standard eight-hour workday for all workers in the United States. Throughout the early 1900s, railroad workers' wages were typically 25 to 30 percent higher than those of workers in other industries. Despite this advantage, railroad unions continued to press for and receive pay increases as well as other benefits.

After World War II, railroad traffic declined dramatically—a result of growing competition from automobiles, trucks, and planes—and the number of railroad workers fell as well. Even so, rail workers still enjoyed good pay and other benefits. Railroad unions also succeeded in keeping the size of train crews constant until recent years—though certain crew members, such as firemen, were not needed on modern trains. The jobs of these employees were protected by work rules clauses in union contracts. With the decline in train service, the unions have gradually allowed some work rules to be dropped.

Minority Workers. Minorities, particularly Chinese and African Americans, played a notable role in the history of U.S. railroads. During the 1800s thousands of Chinese laborers helped lay tracks in the West. After the tracks were completed, however, few Chinese continued to work for the railroads.

Meanwhile, after the Civil War, newly freed African Americans began to find jobs on the railroad. At first the railroads hired blacks only if they were needed to break labor strikes by white workers. At the same time, union contracts often called for limiting the number of African Americans who could be employed. The first wide-scale working opportunities for blacks came in 1867 with the founding of the Pullman Palace Car Company, which hired them to serve as porters.

Porters toiled long hours under terrible conditions for very low wages. Other African American railroad workers had low-paying jobs and poor working conditions as well. Moreover, racial prejudice greatly limited their opportunities for advancement. Black railroad workers had to look out for themselves because they generally were not welcome in the established labor unions.

The Chinese Connection

When the first transcontinental railroad in the United States was laid in the 1860s, the builders had a difficult time finding labor in the West. Many men had gone to California to find fortune in gold mines, not to work on railroads. Officials for the Central Pacific Railroad decided to try using Chinese immigrants. Few believed that the Chinese, who tended to be slightly built, could handle the heavy work. But they proved to be excellent workers, and the railroad began to recruit them directly in China. When the second transcontinental railroad was built in the 1880s, more than 12,000 Chinese laborers took part in its construction.

The first African American railroad union was the Association of Colored Railway Trainmen and Locomotive Firemen, founded in 1913. During World War I, two more black unions arose, the most important of which was the Sleeping Car Porters Protective Union. During the 1930s this union opened its membership to baggage handlers—redcaps—as well as to maids and other sleeping car employees. By the 1970s black and white railroad workers had become integrated, and they enjoyed the same benefits. *See also* Labor Unions; Pullman Strike; Railroad Industry; Railroads, History of; Randolph, A. Philip; Transcontinental Railroad.

Railway Stations

facilities something built or created to serve a particular function

With the development of railroads, it became necessary to provide **facilities** at train stops and at the end of train lines for sheltering passengers and storing cargo. This led to the establishment of official railway stations, where most railroad activities were centered.

The earliest railroad stations in the United States were little more than sheds placed along the sides of railroad tracks. These early stations were called depots because they served as places where passengers gathered and goods were deposited until the next train came along. Early railway depots offered no luxuries and most lacked basic facilities such as restrooms or even places to sit. Often the railroads simply took over abandoned stagecoach offices, old houses, or other buildings and used them as depots.

Although usually not impressive buildings, railway depots became the center of activity in small towns across the United States. They attracted people of all ages who wanted a taste of the excitement and romance of the railroad and a link to the outside world. Townsfolk went to the depot to ship packages, send messages by telegraph, find newspapers from other towns, and meet visitors passing through.

The station agent, the official railroad representative, was often one of the town's leading citizens. In addition to their railroad duties, agents might also serve as postmasters, florists, salesmen, and even barbers or dentists.

As railroad passenger travel increased so did the need for larger railway stations with more facilities and services for passengers. The first large station designed specifically for passengers was the Old Colony and Newport Depot, built in Boston in 1847. It featured an elegant waiting room, barbershop, newsstand, restrooms, and ladies' sitting room, among other comforts. However, railway stations generally remained just a place to stop the train until after the Civil War.

During the 1870s and 1880s, elaborately designed stations began to spring up in towns and cities of all sizes. Though building styles varied and might include fancy exterior decoration with columns and towers, inside most stations just provided basic comforts such as seating areas and washrooms. Urban stations, however, often offered much more.

From 1875 to 1925 many monumental railway stations were built in American cities. Among the most impressive were Penn Station and Grand Central Terminal in New York. These magnificent buildings, which opened in 1910 and 1913 respectively, featured exclusive shops, restaurants, and other services. Grand Central Terminal even had a

Union Station in Washington, D.C., built in 1908, was modeled after the Baths of Diocletian in Rome.

gymnasium and washrooms with showers, tubs, and dressing rooms. These stations were like small cities, employing thousands of people and serving many thousands of travelers each day.

The decline of the railroads after World War II had a dramatic effect on railroad stations. Many large ones fell into disrepair, and most small-town stations were closed. Modern commuter train stations are typically small and simple in design, with few passenger comforts. However, a number of grand railway stations in large cities have been restored since the 1980s—offering reminders of a time when the train was a symbol of romance and excitement. *See also* PASSENGERS; RAILROAD INDUSTRY; RAILROADS, HISTORY OF.

Railway Trains, Parts of

Locomotives, freight cars, and passenger cars—known as rolling stock—are the basic parts of railway trains. In addition, trains are equipped with various devices and mechanisms that make them safer and more comfortable, including brakes and couplers that connect the railroad cars.

Locomotives

Locomotives supply power to move trains. They may run on steam, electricity, or diesel fuel. The earliest steam-powered locomotives, introduced in the 1820s, could travel about 30 miles (48 km) per hour. Although

The wheels of a steam locomotive are driven by moving pistons, which are powered by steam produced in the boilers.

piston mechanical part moved back and forth by fluid pressure inside a chamber

enormously improved over the next hundred years, steam locomotives have gradually been replaced in most areas of the world by more efficient diesel and electric models. The fastest trains in service today can reach speeds of 300 miles (483 km) per hour.

A steam locomotive is basically a large boiler. By burning coal or wood to heat the water in the boiler, or firebox, steam is produced. The pressure of the steam causes the engine's **pistons** to move. The pistons are connected by rods to large wheels beneath the locomotive, and their movement turns these wheels and drives the train.

The electric locomotive, first used by the Baltimore and Ohio Railroad in 1895, does not supply its own power. It runs on electricity provided through an overhead wire or an electrified third rail on the tracks. The electric power travels from overhead wires to the train through a pantograph, a device on the roof of the locomotive. With third rails, the electric current is transmitted through a mechanism called a shoe, which slides along the rail beneath the locomotive. The current must be converted (by a transformer and rectifier) into a form that can be used by the locomotive's motor so that it can drive the wheels of the train.

Diesel locomotives were introduced in the 1920s. One type, diesel-electric, has an oil-burning diesel engine that supplies power to an electric generator. The generator produces electricity, which runs the motors that drive the wheels of the locomotive. In another type, the diesel-hydraulic locomotive, the engine's power is transmitted to the driving mechanisms by fluids under high pressure.

All locomotives have cabs, where the engineer sits. The cab contains the instruments used to operate the train, to receive information about track and traffic conditions, and to send signals.

Freight Cars

From the earliest days of railroading, trains served as a means for hauling heavy loads quickly and conveniently. The cargo carried by trains has changed considerably over the years, and freight cars have also changed to meet new needs.

Early freight cars were little more than wooden boxes with railroad wheels attached to fixed axles. It was soon discovered that such cars had a tendency to tip over when rounding curves or traveling above certain speeds. Railroads replaced the fixed axles with "trucks" or "bogies"— units containing two or more axles that could swivel beneath the cars. These trucks soon became standard on all railway cars and locomotives, reducing accidents and making railroad travel more comfortable.

Three basic types of freight cars have been in use since the 1800s: open-top cars, boxcars, and flatcars.

Open-Top Cars. Open-top cars called hoppers are used to haul bulk freight such as coal, gravel, or grain. Most contain either a hatch or a collapsible bottom for the fast unloading of cargo. A gondola car has a fixed bottom and must be unloaded from the top with a crane. The side walls of some gondolas are built in separate sections that can slide over one another, allowing one portion of the car to be unloaded without exposing the rest of the cargo. Gondolas often carry manufactured goods. Movable covers are sometimes used on open-top cars to protect cargo from the weather.

Boxcars. Most boxcars are fully enclosed cars with sliding doors on either side. They are used primarily to haul manufactured goods that must be protected from the weather or from theft. The entire sidewall of modern boxcars is divided into several doors for easy unloading. On some boxcars, the sidewalls are replaced with a framework that can be moved aside to reveal the whole interior of the car. Special-purpose boxcars include refrigerated cars for transporting fresh or frozen foods and stock cars—boxcars with slatted sides that carry livestock.

Flatcars. Flatcars are basically flat metal platforms mounted on train wheels. The cargo, often heavy equipment, is strapped down with ropes or chains. Since the 1950s several types of specialized flatcars, such as container cars and piggyback cars, have appeared.

Container cars are designed to transport the standard-sized shipping containers that now carry the bulk of cargo worldwide. Packed before shipping, the containers can be quickly loaded or unloaded from a flatcar, eliminating the need to pack individual items into a boxcar.

Piggyback cars can haul truck trailers, which are simply disconnected from the truck cab and lifted into place on the car. When the train reaches its destination, the trailers are unloaded, hooked up to truck cabs, and driven away.

Other Types of Freight Cars. A number of other specialized freight cars are designed to transport particular types of cargo. Tank cars, really just large tanks on railroad wheels, haul liquids such as oil,

Railway Cars
Diesel-Electric Locomotive

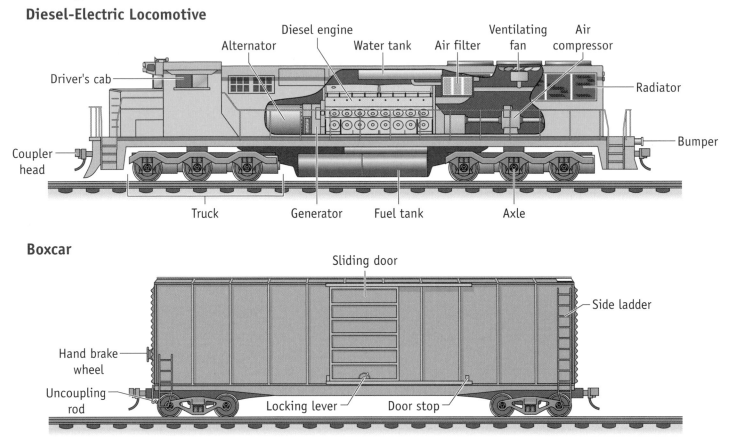

Boxcar

Freight trains consist of locomotives and various freight cars, such as the boxcar illustrated here.

sensor device that reacts to changes in light, heat, motion, and so on

water, or chemicals. Specially lined tank cars are used for wine, corn syrup, or other liquids that should not come in contact with the tanks' metal walls.

Triple-deck freight cars with movable ramps transport automobiles. These freight cars have flaps that can be extended to form a single ramp running the length of the train. Automobiles can then be driven off the train instead of being unloaded by a crane.

One type of freight car is fading into railroad history. The caboose, once occupied by the brakeman who stopped the train, is rapidly disappearing. Modern trains have air brakes. Electronic **sensors** at the end of the train send signals to the locomotive, where the engineer monitors and controls brake pressure. This system has eliminated the need for a caboose.

Passenger Cars

Even at the height of rail travel in the early 1900s, passenger cars represented only a fraction of all railway cars. Nevertheless, the railroads devoted a great deal of time and effort to adding comfort and even luxury to passenger cars and to producing cars specifically designed for activities such as dining and viewing the scenery. The most common passenger cars, however, have always been coaches and sleeping cars.

Coaches. The earliest passenger cars were small wooden coaches like those used on roads, but they had special wheels adapted to railway tracks. By the 1870s railroads in both the United States and Europe had developed larger passenger cars, some capable of holding up to 40 passengers.

Most early passenger coaches had a similar design: a central aisle with rows of benches on either side. During the 1800s these coaches became increasingly comfortable as wooden benches gave way to padded seats. Eventually most European coaches had closed compartments seating six to eight people with a corridor running along the side of the coach. European railroads also established three separate classes of passenger travel. In the United States, trains generally have had only a single class.

Modern passenger coaches are quite comfortable and provide travelers with many conveniences, including restrooms and telephone service. Some have audio systems with headphones at each seat and even video screens. Outlets for laptop computers have been added on some trains for the convenience of business travelers. Certain trains include separate dining cars, lounge cars, and observation cars.

Sleeper Cars. Long-distance train travel created a need for overnight accommodations. The first car with berths for sleeping was put into service in 1837 on the Cumberland Valley Railroad of Pennsylvania. However, the accommodations were crude—just a rough mattress and pillow. A sleeping car equipped with hinged upper berths that could be pushed up against the wall during the day and swung down for sleeping at night was introduced in 1856.

Most sleeping cars have seats that can be converted into beds. More deluxe versions consist of a private sleeping compartment, such as the one shown here, with its own bathroom.

American inventor George Pullman traveled on a train with one of the new sleeping cars. He found himself tossed about so much that he decided to design his own sleeping car. Pullman enlarged the size of berths and reinforced the car's wheel truck with rubber cushions to improve the ride. The use of rubber cushions was soon adopted for all types of passenger cars. Pullman sleeping cars were put into service in the 1860s, and they became known for comfort. Many prominent individuals ordered luxurious Pullman coaches for their business and personal travel.

Most modern sleeping cars have seats that can be converted into beds, as well as additional beds that fold up out of sight when not in use. Some double-decker sleeping cars have regular sleeping compartments as well as family rooms, lounges, and even shower rooms that allow travelers to bathe while aboard the train.

Brakes, Couplers, and Wheels

Locomotives, freight cars, and passenger cars have a variety of devices and mechanisms to increase safety, improve operating efficiency, and increase passenger comfort. Many of these devices are automated, programmed by computer.

One of the most important parts of a train is the braking system. In the early days of railroading, the brakeman moved through a train setting the brakes of each car by hand. Modern trains have automatic braking systems: the brakes of each car are operated through an electronic control system. The stopping force in the brakes is provided by compressed air.

The coupling system is another important element in railroads. Couplers are mechanisms that connect cars to form a train. For many years, workers had to go from car to car operating the couplers manually. Modern trains have automatic couplers that are integrated with the braking system. If cars become uncoupled while moving, the brakes are applied automatically.

The wheels of railroad cars are joined by axles. On older cars, the ends of these axles rotated against a solid surface enclosed in a metal box. Friction often caused the box to become overheated, creating a "hotbox." If the box became too hot, the axle could actually burn away and the wheels would fall off. Modern rail cars have rollers at the end of axles, instead of a solid surface, which helps prevent hotboxes. In addition, electronic devices called hotbox detectors can sense overheating in the wheels.

The front ends of locomotives and railroad cars are known as trucks—movable units containing two or more axles and sets of wheels. These sections allow the cars to swivel slightly when going around curves. Some modern, high-speed passenger trains automatically tilt as they travel around curves. Special devices in the front of the train respond to signals from electronic sensors, which react to curves in the track. The tilt systems are designed to provide greater safety and comfort. *See also* Auto Train; Containerization; Engines; Freight Trains; High-Speed Trains; Light Rail Systems; Passengers; Railroad Industry; Railroads, History of; Railway Trains, Types of; Subways (Metros).

The Real McCoy

Early locomotives had a serious problem with wear and tear caused by the constant friction of parts grinding against each other. The problem was solved by an African American engineer named Elijah McCoy. Educated in Scotland, McCoy was forced to take a menial job with the Michigan Central Railroad because of his race. In 1870, while working as a railroad fireman, he invented a device that enabled workers to lubricate machines without stopping them. The device became so important that users referred to it as "the real McCoy." McCoy held more than 50 patents for his inventions and his lubricating systems are now used all over the world.

Railway Trains, Types of

Further Information
To learn more about railroad history, the railroad industry, the parts of a train, and specific types of trains, see the related articles listed at the end of this entry.

piston *mechanical part moved back and forth by fluid pressure inside a chamber*

Railway trains come in a variety of types and have different functions. They can be classified according to the service the train offers, such as passenger or freight transportation, or they can be classified by the type of engine that drives the train, such as a steam, diesel, or electric locomotive.

Types of Locomotives

Locomotives provide the power needed to push or pull trains. The early railroads used steam locomotives, but diesel fuel and electricity have replaced steam as sources of power for trains in most areas of the world.

Steam Locomotives. A steam locomotive is basically a large boiler heated by burning coal. The steam it produces supplies the power to drive the train. The steam engines of the early 1800s could pull just a few cars and travel only about 20 miles (32 km) per hour. As technology advanced, engineers developed steam locomotives that could pull 200-car trains at speeds up to 75 miles (121 km) per hour.

Steam locomotives are simple and durable, but they have several drawbacks. They require frequent servicing, even after relatively short runs, and their wheels, driven by moving **pistons,** place a great deal of stress on the railroad tracks. The pounding motion of the wheels can cause kinks and bend the rails. Burning coal to heat the boiler produces large amounts of air pollution. In addition, steam engines are quite inefficient, converting only about 6 percent of the heat energy generated by the boiler into usable power.

Diesel Locomotives. The invention of the diesel engine in the late 1800s revolutionized locomotive design. At the time, diesel fuel was cheaper than coal, and diesel engines were four times more efficient than steam engines. They also were cleaner. Compared to steam engines, diesels could accelerate faster and operate at higher speeds without damaging tracks, and they could run for longer periods without maintenance. Furthermore, diesel engine designs were standardized, which meant that repair parts were cheap and easy to obtain. By the end of World War II, 27,000 diesel locomotives had replaced the 40,000 steam-powered models in the United States.

Most diesel locomotives today use a diesel engine to supply power to an electric motor that drives the wheels. They are known as diesel-electric locomotives. The electric motor provides power more smoothly and evenly than a steam or diesel engine, enabling the train to accelerate and brake with little or no wheel slippage. The drive wheels, which are not attached to pistons, cause less damage to the track. The vast majority of modern locomotives are diesel-electric.

Electric Locomotives. Electric locomotives do not supply their own power. Instead, they use electricity generated elsewhere and convert it into energy to drive the train. This external power supply allows electric locomotives to draw additional energy when needed for hauling heavy loads or going up steep hills. A steam or diesel locomotive is limited to the amount of power its own engine can produce.

In the late 1800s and early 1900s, engineers developed several types of passenger railway trains that ran on electricity. Els, elevated railroad lines built on platforms above city streets, used an electric power source. Electric streetcars or trolleys were equipped with a long pole with a small wheel on the end that drew electricity from an overhead wire. Trams are the modern versions of these vehicles. Monorails run on a single electric-powered rail. Electric subways operate in underground transportation systems in some large cities. In the 1980s and 1990s, high-speed trains capable of reaching speeds of more than 300 miles (483 km) per hour began to appear. These railway systems receive electricity from an overhead line.

The external power source is also the main drawback to electric locomotives. Installing overhead electric lines or long sections of electrified track is expensive, so the amount of rail traffic must be great enough to justify the cost. As a result, electric locomotives are found mostly in subways and commuter rail lines or in small countries where distances are not great. Japan and some European nations use electricity to power many of their trains. More than 99 percent of the rail lines in Switzerland are electrified. In the United States, on the other hand, only about 1 percent of all rail lines are electrified; most of these are located in the heavily populated northeastern states.

Many European nations have electric trains. In the United States, however, only about 1 percent of all rail lines are electrified.

Other Types of Trains. Some train cars, known as railcars, are not pulled by a locomotive. Instead, these cars have a built-in power unit, often an electric or diesel-electric engine. Other railway trains do not run on steam, diesel, or electric power. Air-cushion vehicles, also known as hovercraft or ground-effect machines, travel on a compressed layer of air. "Maglev" trains employ magnets that are placed underneath the train and allow it to float over a guide rail.

Types of Service

Railway trains provide passenger or freight service, or a combination of the two. They also offer special services, such as intermodal transportation, to meet customers' needs.

Passenger Service. Intercity coaches, high-speed trains, and subways or metros all serve passengers. Usually located in or between cities, these trains offer fast transportation over short or long distances. They also provide an essential means of moving people between cities and their suburbs. In the United States trains carry less than 1 percent of intercity passenger traffic, but in Europe and other parts of the world, railroads remain an important form of passenger travel.

Freight Service. Freight trains are the most common type of trains riding the rails today. Because of their efficient use of fuel, freight trains can compete successfully with trucking companies, airfreight services, and watercraft for cargo, especially bulk goods.

Intermodal Service. Some railroads offer intermodal service, a system that incorporates two or more modes of transportation in one journey. Intermodal passenger trains allow customers to combine motor vehicle and train travel. They include special cars designed to carry passengers' automobiles. Intermodal freight trains carry goods packed in large containers that can be transferred to trucks or ships as needed. *See also* AIR-CUSHION VEHICLES; AUTO TRAIN; ENGINES; FREIGHT TRAINS; HIGH-SPEED TRAINS; INTERMODAL TRANSPORT; LIGHT RAIL SYSTEMS; PASSENGERS; RAILROAD INDUSTRY; RAILROADS, HISTORY OF; RAILWAY TRAINS, PARTS OF; SUBWAYS (METROS).

Randolph, A. Philip

American labor leader

socialist *relating to socialism, a system in which the production and distribution of goods are controlled by the state*

A. Philip Randolph organized the Brotherhood of Sleeping Car Porters (BSCP), the first all-black labor union. His efforts on behalf of African American workers in the railroad industry and other areas led to their winning important rights and recognition by labor unions.

Born in 1889, in Crescent City, Florida, Randolph was the son of a Methodist minister. After attending City College of New York, he joined the **socialist** movement. Convinced that labor unions were the key to improving the wages of African Americans, Randolph began trying to organize blacks working on New York and New Jersey docks. In 1917 he cofounded the *Messenger,* a radical newspaper for blacks. When a group of railroad porters asked him to lead a union on their behalf, he formed the BSCP in 1925.

Serving as president of the BSCP, Randolph became a noted labor leader. At a time when most blacks were barred from trade unions, the BSCP was admitted into the American Federation of Labor (AFL). The brotherhood later gained recognition from the Pullman company, which built sleeping cars and operated them on behalf of the railroads. However, in 1937, Randolph moved the BSCP to the Congress of Industrial Organizations (CIO) to protest the AFL's lack of progress in fighting racial discrimination within its ranks. When the AFL and the CIO merged in 1955, Randolph became a vice president of the new labor federation, giving him a stronger position from which to reform the practices of labor unions.

Randolph won significant gains for African American workers in the federal government as well. In 1941 he threatened to organize a mass march on Washington, D.C., on behalf of blacks seeking equal employment in the federal government and the defense industry. To prevent a major disturbance in the country, President Franklin Roosevelt issued an executive order prohibiting discrimination in hiring by federal departments and the defense industry. Roosevelt also created the Fair Employment Practices Committee. In 1948 Randolph played a part in convincing President Harry Truman to issue an executive order banning discrimination in the armed forces. Randolph stepped down from the presidency of the BSCP in 1968 and died in 1979. *See also* Labor Unions; Railroad Workers.

Recreational Vehicles (RVs)

Recreational vehicles (RVs) are wheeled structures that provide temporary living space, enabling travelers to enjoy the comforts of home while on the road. There are two types of RVs: motor vehicles with their own engine and steering system; and trailers that must be towed or hauled by another vehicle using a hitch. RVs were introduced in the 1920s, and their popularity boomed during and after the 1960s.

RVs can contain a wide range of features including beds, refrigerators, stoves, toilets, and sinks, as well as storage space for water, fuel, and waste. When not on the road, RVs may stop at trailer parks that provide connections to water and electricity. However, most RVs are self-contained units that can function for long periods without these connections.

Motorized RVs, known as motor homes, can measure up to 40 feet (12 m) long and 8½ feet (3 m) wide. The largest models may have several separate rooms and can sleep up to ten people. The van camper and van conversion, modified vans with RV features such as sleeping space and carpeting, are related vehicles.

Trailer RVs come in several forms. The park trailer is the largest type and is designed for use as a seasonal or permanent home in a trailer park. Travel trailers resemble motor homes in size and features. The folding camping trailer has canvas extensions that open up like a tent for sleeping and then collapse into a small rectangular trailer for travel. The truck camper, another compact type of RV, is hauled on the back of a pickup truck. *See also* Mobile Homes.

Regulation of Transportation

Further Information
To learn more about regulation of transportation, including government agencies and legislation regarding motor vehicles, trains, ships, and airplanes, see the related articles listed at the end of this entry.

monopoly *control of a market or product by a single company or country*

Airlines, railroads, trucking companies, and other transportation providers play such an important role in modern society that virtually all countries have taken steps to control their activities. Government regulations deal with matters such as passenger fares, freight rates, and safety.

Regulation Policies and Procedures

Safety is a primary goal of transportation regulations. Ships, trains, buses, and airplanes carry large numbers of people who might be seriously injured or killed if an accident occurs. Regulations often specify safety and maintenance procedures and equipment requirements that transportation companies must follow.

Government legislation and regulations also protect customers against unfair business practices. In the past, for example, the U.S. government adopted rules to prevent railroads from charging unreasonably high rates in areas where they had a **monopoly.** Policies that encourage competition in a particular industry are designed to safeguard passenger fares and freight rates and to make the industry more efficient. Other government regulations outline the transportation providers' legal and financial responsibilities to their customers, which can be enforced by the courts.

Regulatory Agencies, Laws, and Agreements.
Legislation forms the basis for government control of transportation. Laws can be used to establish operating procedures, set safety standards, and create regulatory agencies to monitor transportation providers.

In the United States, government agencies often set industry-wide standards for safety, pricing, and performance. They may inspect vehicles and equipment, authorize rate changes, or collect information about the efficiency or reliability of transportation services. Public agencies also assume responsibility for matters that are beyond the scope of individual businesses, such as weather forecasting, air traffic control, and highway construction. The goal is to make transportation systems safe, efficient, and fair. The Department of Transportation monitors many aspects of transportation. Within the department, agencies such as the Federal Railroad Administration, Federal Aviation Administration (FAA), and Federal Highway Administration regulate specific forms of transportation.

International agreements cover transportation providers that carry people and goods between countries. The Berne Convention, for example, which regulates the shipment of freight by rail across national borders, was signed by various European nations in 1890 and has been updated several times since then. The International Civil Aviation Organization (ICAO) sets worldwide standards for aircraft operation. Virtually all countries belong to the ICAO, which is an agency of the United Nations.

Deregulation.
Meeting government standards sometimes raises the cost of transportation. The increased costs can make industries less profitable and discourage competition. This occurred with U.S. railroads in the 1950s and 1960s.

Government agencies regulate many aspects of the transportation industry in the United States, from safety procedures and training to equipment and pollution control.

U.S. Regulatory Agencies

Department of Transportation

U.S. Coast Guard	Maritime Administration (MARAD)
Federal Aviation Administration (FAA)	National Highway Traffic Safety Administration
Federal Transit Administration	St. Lawrence Seaway Development Corporation
Federal Highway Administration (FHWA)	Federal Railroad Administration (FRA)

Other Regulatory Bodies

Environmental Protection Agency (EPA)	National Aeronautics and Space Administration (NASA)
National Transportation Safety Board (NTSB)	Federal Trade Commission (FTC)
Federal Trade Commission (FTC)	

Over the long term, such problems may affect an entire industry, creating opposition to certain government controls. As a result, various transportation industries in the United States have been deregulated—government controls have been reduced or eliminated—over the years. Restrictions on American railroads, for example, were eased in 1980 by the Staggers Rail Act.

Maritime Regulations

Laws relating to ships and shipping represent a very early form of transportation regulation. The practices of seagoing traders from Egypt, Phoenicia, and Greece probably formed the basis for the first known set of **maritime** laws, compiled before 300 B.C. by the people of the island of Rhodes. This code influenced the emperor Justinian, who wrote maritime laws for ancient Rome.

During the Middle Ages, European seaports developed codes that provided the foundation for modern law on ships and shipping. The Laws of Oleron, a French code, had a significant effect on the policies of a number of other nations. By the 1300s maritime courts had emerged in England to decide questions concerning naval vessels. Their authority was later expanded to include commercial shipping. During the 1600s the British set up maritime courts in the American colonies. After the American Revolution, the U.S. Congress passed the Judiciary Act of 1789, which gave the federal courts authority over maritime law.

Modern governments continue to regulate many aspects of shipping, including freight and passenger rates, the registration of vessels, and

maritime related to the sea or shipping

working conditions of ships' crews. In the United States, the Maritime Administration oversees such matters on behalf of the Department of Transportation. The U.S. Coast Guard inspects ships and enforces maritime laws.

Over the years a number of international agreements have been made to avoid conflicts between the maritime laws of individual countries. In 1889 international rules for prevention of collisions at sea were adopted. Since 1914 the International Convention for Safety of Life at Sea has issued various sets of guidelines regarding ship construction, lifesaving devices, radio equipment, and other safety measures. Since 1958 the Inter-Governmental Maritime Consultative Organization, a United Nations agency, has worked to promote international cooperation on maritime matters. Besides safety and navigation, other areas of international concern include marine pollution, insurance, and **salvage** operations in case of an accident.

salvage saving or recovering property lost underwater

Railroad Regulations

Railroads are important not only to the economy of a country but also to the movement of troops and military supplies. For these reasons governments often either own and operate or heavily regulate the railroads. In France all the country's railroads have been run by the government since 1938. One of Canada's two major freight lines, Canadian National Railways, was government owned for many years, but is now a private corporation. Nearly all the railroads in the United States are privately owned, except for the passenger rail service, Amtrak, which receives some public funding. American railroads have operated under strict federal guidelines since the early 1900s, though regulations have been eased in recent years.

Government regulation and control of railroads arose as a result of unfair business practices among some early rail companies, such as granting special rates to preferred customers. Regulation began in Britain in 1830 with the Carriers Act, which applied to both road and railroad freight companies. In later years Parliament passed laws, such as the Railways Act of 1921, specifically governing railroads. As train service expanded across national borders, governments also developed international policy concerning rail transport. The Berne Convention, mentioned above, established standards for freight train service within Europe, including rules regarding damage to cargo or delays in delivery.

Regulating U.S. Railroads. In the United States, Congress passed the Interstate Commerce Act in 1887, which gave the Interstate Commerce Commission (ICC) the power to regulate railroads. A series of acts passed during the early 1900s strengthened the ICC's authority over railroad rates and labor disputes.

Tight government regulations on passenger fares, freight rates, and mergers, however, helped weaken U.S. railroads when they were already facing increasing competition from other modes of transportation, including cars, trucks, and airlines. Railroads struggled for decades under the double burden of declining business and stiff federal rules. Many rail lines either merged or went into bankruptcy, until the mid-1900s, when the government began to ease regulations. The 1980 Staggers Rail Act, for example, loosened ICC control over railroad rates to help increase company profits. In 1996 the ICC was abolished and most of its responsibilities were taken over by the Department of Transportation.

Highway and Motor Vehicle Regulation

The regulation of motor vehicle transportation covers two broad areas—highways and vehicles. Governments around the world have enacted laws concerning highway design and use and have established requirements for motor vehicle safety inspections, licensing, fuel mileage standards, and pollution controls.

Highways. In the United States the growing importance of the automobile throughout the twentieth century created a need for an extensive and well-organized network of roads. Under acts passed in 1916 and 1921, Congress set aside funds for road building in rural areas. Legislation of 1956 established the U.S. Interstate Highway System, a massive road-building program with federal guidelines for funding, road design, routes, and numbering of roadways.

Over the years Congress has passed additional laws expanding the size of the highway system and providing further funding for construction and improvements. The Transportation Equity Act for the Twenty-first Century, passed in 1998, included more than $23 billion for interstate highway maintenance.

Motor Vehicles. Among the earliest laws aimed at regulating automobiles was the Motor Car Act, passed in Britain in 1903 to establish safety standards for London taxicabs. American carmakers, however, operated with little government oversight until the 1960s, when the safety and efficient operation of cars became major public concerns.

The National Traffic and Motor Vehicle Safety Act of 1966 was one of the first U.S. laws aimed at making cars safer to drive. Over the years the government has required manufacturers to install seat belts, improved bumpers and brakes, air bags, and other safety devices on all cars sold in the United States.

Pollution control and energy efficiency of cars also became important issues in the 1960s. Many of the big American-made cars produced large amounts of **pollutants** and used more gasoline than smaller cars. The Vehicle Air Pollution and Control Act of 1965 and the Clean Air Act of 1970 attempted to reduce automobile **emissions.**

Gasoline prices rose in the United States during a series of oil shortages in the 1970s, creating a need for smaller, more fuel-efficient cars. Drivers began to purchase foreign-made cars, which tended to be relatively small and have good gas mileage because of the high cost of fuel overseas. To force American automakers to improve the fuel efficiency of their cars, Congress passed the Energy Policy and Conservation Act in 1975. The law set minimum gasoline mileage standards for each

Government Roads

In the early 1900s, most roads in the United States were unpaved. People living in rural areas were especially unhappy with the condition of the roads and put pressure on the government to improve them.

In 1916 Congress passed the Federal-Aid Road Act, authorizing $75 million for highway construction. To receive funding, the individual states had to contribute matching funds of their own and build the roads to federal standards. The act provided the foundation for future government regulation of highway building in the United States.

pollutant *something that contaminates the environment*

emissions *substances discharged into the air*

manufacturer's product line that were to be met over a period of years. The standards were relaxed during the 1980s as part of a general trend toward deregulation of industry.

New legislation has continued to increase safety standards and environmental guidelines. For example, the Clean Air Act of 1990 gave the federal government the right to set stricter limits on vehicle emissions. That same year the California Air Resources Board declared that 10 percent of new vehicles sold in California by 2003 must be zero-emission vehicles. The Transportation Equity Act for the Twenty-first Century, enacted in 1998, included provisions to fight drunk driving, promote child safety seat use, improve truck safety, and purchase buses that use low-polluting fuels.

Airline Regulations

The first law governing air travel was enacted in 1908, just five years after the Wright brothers' pioneer flight. The residents of Kissimmee, Florida, set guidelines on speed and altitude for pilots flying over their community. Three years later Connecticut passed a law requiring pilots to have a license.

As airline service grew, both national and international regulations were adopted. In the international arena, the basic principle that each nation has control of its own **airspace** was established in 1919 at the Paris Convention on the Regulation of Aerial Navigation. Under this agreement, airlines of one country must receive permission to fly into the airspace of another. Other international agreements include the 1928 Havana Convention, which standardized ticket and baggage handling

airspace *space above a certain area of land or water; also, space lying above and controlled by a nation*

Various government agencies in the United States establish standards for safety, performance, and pollution control in transportation. The Federal Aviation Administration (FAA) sets standards for aircraft manufacture and operation.

procedures, and the 1929 Warsaw Convention on International Carriage by Air, which limited an airline company's liability when passengers are injured or killed in aviation accidents.

Governments of virtually all countries regulate aviation and airlines in some way. In the United States, the Air Commerce Act of 1926 established the first federal regulations for the aviation industry. The Civil Aeronautics Board (CAB), organized in 1938, was given control over airline rates, routes, and mergers. The Federal Aviation Administration (FAA), set up in 1958, operates air traffic control centers and has broad powers over aviation safety, including licensing of pilots, rules of air navigation, and certification of airplane design and manufacture.

Until the late 1970s, federal regulation of the airline industry was extensive. However, experiments with easing government control indicated that allowing airlines to set their own fares and routes could improve efficiency and performance. In 1978 Congress passed the Airline Deregulation Act, loosening federal controls. By 1984 Congress had ended the CAB's regulatory authority over airlines and dissolved the agency, placing responsibility for monitoring airline service with the Department of Transportation. *See also* AIRLINE INDUSTRY; AIR TRAFFIC CONTROL; AUTOMOBILES; CIVIL AERONAUTICS BOARD; DRIVING; FAA; GOVERNMENT AND TRANSPORTATION; INTERSTATE COMMERCE COMMISSION; MARITIME LAW; NATIONAL TRANSPORTATION SAFETY BOARD; RAILROADS, HISTORY OF; ROADS; SHIPS AND BOATS, SAFETY OF; TRADE AND COMMERCE; TRANSPORTATION, U.S. DEPARTMENT OF.

Rickshaws

see Carts, Carriages, and Wagons.

Ride, Sally
American astronaut

NASA National Aeronautics and Space Administration, the U.S. space agency

American astronaut Sally Kristen Ride was the first American woman to fly in space. Born in 1951 near Los Angeles, California, Ride excelled in athletics, but she gave up a career in tennis to study science and earned a Ph.D. in physics from Stanford University. In 1978 she entered the **NASA** astronaut training program. During her first mission on the space shuttle *Challenger* in June 1983, Ride conducted medical experiments and used the shuttle's robot arm to launch communications satellites. Her second mission took place in October 1984. Ride later served on the presidentially appointed Rogers Commission that investigated the *Challenger* explosion in 1986. After retiring from NASA, she became a professor of physics at the University of California at San Diego and the director of the California Space Institute. *See also* CHALLENGER DISASTER; SPACE SHUTTLES.

Rivers of the World

Long before there were roads and highways, rivers served as routes for fishers, merchants and traders, explorers, and armies. Over the centuries great advances have been made in land and air transportation, but the world's major rivers still carry an enormous amount of cargo as well as passenger and recreation vessels. On some rivers, dams and canals have been built to bypass rapids, falls, shallow water, and other obstacles to navigation.

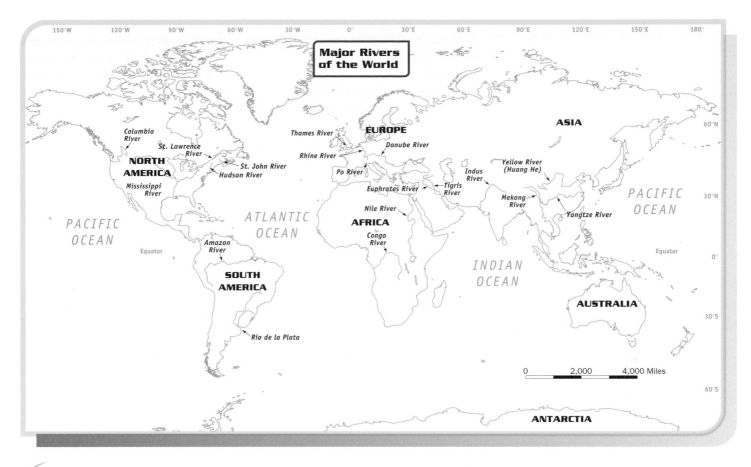

Major Rivers of the World

150°W 120°W 90°W 60°W 30°W 0° 30°E 60°E 90°E 120°E 150°E 180°

ASIA

60°N

Columbia River

Thames River

EUROPE

St. Lawrence River

Rhine River

Danube River

Yellow River (Huang He)

NORTH AMERICA

St. John River

Po River

Indus River

30°N

Hudson River

Euphrates River

Tigris River

Mekong River

PACIFIC OCEAN

Mississippi River

ATLANTIC OCEAN

Nile River

Yangtze River

PACIFIC OCEAN

Equator

Amazon River

AFRICA

Congo River

INDIAN OCEAN

Equator

0°

SOUTH AMERICA

AUSTRALIA

30°S

Rio de la Plata

0   2,000   4,000 Miles

60°S

ANTARCTIA

Rivers continue to serve as important transportation routes around the world.

tributary *stream or river that flows into a larger stream or river*

navigable *deep or wide enough for boats or ships to pass through*

Amazon. Flowing 4,000 miles (6,436 km) from west to east along the equator, the Amazon River is the longest river in South America and the second longest in the world. Its course begins in the Andes of Peru and ends in the Atlantic Ocean on the northern side of Marajó Island. The Amazon and its many **tributaries** form a huge **navigable** network in the heart of the Earth's largest tropical rain forest. Small motorboats, sailboats, and canoes are the craft of choice for travel on the waterway, which serves as the principal means of transport and commerce for most of the people who live along its banks. Large oceangoing tankers and passenger ships can also sail on the Amazon. River traffic reaches its peak between April and August, when water levels are highest. Belém and Manaus, Brazil, are the Amazon's major ports.

Columbia. The Columbia River stretches 1,214 miles (1,953 km) through southeast British Columbia and Oregon and Washington. In the early 1800s, fur traders set up posts along the river and explored much of its length. Many pioneers to Oregon Country endured a hair-raising raft trip down the Columbia as the final stage of the Oregon Trail. Today ocean freighters and barges carry local grain, iron, and forest products to the river's mouth on the Pacific Ocean. Although used primarily for transportation, the Columbia is also a critical source of water power.

Congo. Located in Central Africa, the Congo River is more than 2,700 miles (4,344 km) long. Like the Amazon, the Congo is the main route for travel and communication in the region it runs through. With its tributaries, the river offers 8,700 miles (14,000 km) of navigable waterways. Beginning in the late 1400s, European explorers used the Congo to reach Central Africa. Rapids and falls interrupted travel on some sections of the river until the late 1800s, when railroads were built to avoid these obstacles. Modern cargo vessels, passenger boats, and small watercraft gather at Kinshasa, the river's key port.

Danube. The Danube River begins in Germany and flows 1,771 miles (2,850 km) through eastern Europe before emptying into the Black Sea. Along the way are 35 major ports. Despite winter ice and occasional problems with high or low water levels, the Danube carries a large volume of traffic. Cargo ships and barges haul mineral ores, steel, chemicals, and agricultural goods. The Main-Danube Canal links the Danube to the Main River, a tributary of the Rhine, allowing vessels to travel between the Black and North Seas.

Hudson. Although only 306 miles (492 km) long, the Hudson River has been part of one of the most important transportation networks in the United States for centuries. In the 1800s river towns such as Poughkeepsie and Newburgh, New York, used the waterway to send whaling fleets to the Pacific Ocean, and lumberjacks floated timber to sawmills by way of the river. When the Erie Canal was built in 1825, it linked the Hudson to the Great Lakes, speeding the shipment of goods from the west. As a result, New York City, located at the river's mouth, became a center of international trade and immigration.

Indus. The 1,800-mile (2,896-km) Indus River flows from Tibet through Pakistan on its way to the Arabian Sea. Ancient civilizations appeared along the river around 2500 B.C. For thousands of years, the Indus has been used for irrigation. This has lowered its water level and made it navigable only for small craft. Nonetheless, the river served as a trade route until 1878, when a railway was built beside it.

Mekong. The Mekong River runs about 2,600 miles (4,183 km) from Tibet through Southeast Asia to its mouth on the South China Sea. Only the final 350 miles (563 km) are navigable for oceangoing vessels. Parts of the upper Mekong are blocked by rapids and sandbars, although small boats use stretches of the river in Laos for local traffic.

Mississippi. The Mississippi is the main waterway in a system of tributaries that drains all or part of 31 American states and two Canadian provinces. Measuring 2,340 miles (3,765 km) in length, the river rises in Minnesota and flows almost directly south to the Gulf of Mexico. The Missouri, the Mississippi's biggest tributary from the west, and the Ohio, its major tributary from the east, were important transportation routes for settlers and traders during the 1800s. Together the waterways of the Mississippi system offer 15,000 navigable miles (24,135 km).

Various types of watercraft have appeared on the Mississippi over the years: the canoes of the Native Americans and early European explorers; rafts, cargo-hauling flatboats, **keelboats,** and steamboats of the American pioneers; and countless tugboats with blocks of barges today.

Going Against the Flow

Before the introduction of steamships, most goods were carried down the Mississippi River on rafts and flatboats. Strong currents made travel upstream difficult and required the use of keelboats. Mariners guided these narrow craft through the shallows, where the current was weakest. By pushing against the river bottom with poles, the crew members could drive the boats forward. Sometimes the sailors went ashore, put on rope harnesses, and dragged their boats upstream. If they were lucky, they had a mule or ox on hand for the job. Another technique was to loop a rope around a sturdy tree some distance ahead and pull the boat in a process called warping. Occasionally, a boat headed upstream could hoist a sail and get a push from the wind.

keelboat narrow riverboat used to transport freight

Oceangoing freighters and tankers from all parts of the world conduct business in the port of New Orleans, Louisiana. About three-fifths of all commercial shipping in the United States travels on the Mississippi.

Nile. From its source below the equator, the Nile River heads northward through northeastern Africa. The world's longest river completes its 4,160-mile (6,693-km) course at the Mediterranean Sea, where it spreads out into a fan-shaped delta. Formed by three main streams—the Blue Nile, the Atbara, and the White Nile—the Nile has been a highway for local peoples for thousands of years. Egypt's Nile Valley was home to various ancient civilizations that cultivated farmland made fertile by the river's yearly floods. Today the Nile irrigates about 6 million acres (2.43 million hectares) of land in Egypt and about 2.75 million acres (1.1 million hectares) in Sudan. The river is navigable from the delta to the Aswân High Dam, 600 miles (965 km) to the south.

Plata. The Río de la Plata is not a river but a funnel-shaped bay that cuts into the southeast coast of South America between Argentina and Uruguay. Despite strong currents and shifting sandbars, two important

The Nile, the world's longest river, has been a highway for people for thousands of years. The river is navigable from its delta on the Mediterranean Sea to the Aswân High Dam in Egypt for 600 miles (960 km).

harbors—Buenos Aires in Argentina and Montevideo in Uruguay—are located on the Plata. The Paraná and Uruguay Rivers empty into the Río de la Plata.

silt soil suspended and carried in water

Po.   Italy's longest river, the Po, flows 405 miles (652 km) from the western Alps to the Adriatic Sea. **Silt** deposited by floods has made the Po Valley fertile and attracted many invaders to the region over the centuries. Major centers along the Po include the cities of Turin, Piacenza, and Cremona. The stretch of river between Turin and the Adriatic coast is navigable by large freight-carrying ships.

Rhine.   Western Europe's major waterway passes through Switzerland, Germany, and the Netherlands to the North Sea. Canals, locks, and dams have tamed its raging course, allowing it to carry a heavy volume of passenger and cargo traffic, especially in industrial districts such as Germany's Ruhr. The Netherlands Rotterdam-Europoort complex at the mouth of the river is the largest port in the world. In addition to its industrial importance, the 820-mile (1,319-km) Rhine has long been admired for its scenic surroundings. Tourist traffic is heaviest on the stretch between Mainz and Bonn, Germany, where the hills are crowned with castles and vineyards.

Ten Long Rivers

Nile	Africa	4,160 miles (6,693 km)
Amazon	South America	4,000 miles (6,436 km)
Yangtze	Asia	3,434 miles (5,525 km)
Yellow (Huang He)	Asia	2,903 miles (4,671 km)
Congo	Africa	2,700 miles (4,344 km)
Mekong	Asia	2,600 miles (4,183 km)
Mississippi	North America	2,340 miles (3,765 km)
Indus	Asia	1,800 miles (2,896 km)
Danube	Europe	1,771 miles (2,850 km)
Columbia	North America	1,214 miles (1,953 km)

St. John.   The St. John River makes its way through the province of New Brunswick in eastern Canada along a route that has earned it the nickname the "Rhine of America." The waterway is 418 miles (673 km) long. Large boats can travel about 85 miles (137 km) upriver from the Bay of Fundy. Small boats can navigate the river for about 200 miles (322 km).

St. Lawrence.   The 760-mile (1,223-km) St. Lawrence River flows east from Lake Ontario to the Gulf of St. Lawrence. Once a highway into the interior of North America for explorers, missionaries, and fur trappers in canoes, the St. Lawrence is now one of the world's busiest commercial waterways. It carries more freight than any other Canadian river and is a major part of the St. Lawrence Seaway. Built in 1959, the seaway includes natural and artificial lakes, canals, dams, locks, and a 186-mile (299-km) stretch of the St. Lawrence River between Montreal and Lake Ontario. The seaway has made it possible for large oceangoing ships to sail between the Atlantic Ocean and the Great Lakes.

Thames.   Beginning in southeastern England, the Thames River runs through the city of London, one of the world's great ports. From London to its mouth near Gravesend on the North Sea, the river is lined with docks for commercial shipping. Barges

The Yangtze River has been a major east-west route for centuries. Half of China's oceangoing trade travels on this river or its tributaries.

junk Chinese ship with sails made of fiber mats

and small steamboats can travel north of London as far as the city of Oxford. Beyond that point only small craft can navigate the river. A flood barrier on the lower Thames protects London from flooding by extra-high tides.

Tigris and Euphrates. The Tigris and Euphrates Rivers formed the border of the region once known as Mesopotamia, home of many ancient civilizations. Although the Tigris and Euphrates are among western Asia's largest rivers, both are too shallow for big boats. Small local craft can travel on the rivers, which also provide water for irrigation and hydroelectric power.

Yangtze. For centuries the Yangtze (also known as the Yangtze Kiang or Chang) River has been China's main east-west transportation route. The longest river in China and the third longest in the world, it extends for 3,434 miles (5,525 km) from Tibet across central China to the port of Shanghai. Thousands of Chinese live on the Yangtze in **junks,** and some of China's most densely populated and industrially important areas lie along the river. Half of all China's oceangoing trade travels on the Yangtze or its tributaries. Large ships can navigate the river 680 miles (1,094 km) upstream to Wuhan, and river steamers can use other sections.

Yellow. The Yellow River—the Huang He or Hwang Ho in Chinese—is northern China's main waterway, with a length of 2,903 miles (4,671 km). The waterway is better known for devastating floods and sudden shifts of its course than for transportation. The upper Yellow flows too swiftly for large ships and the middle and lower stretches are too shallow for them. *See also* BARGES; CANALS; CANOES AND KAYAKS; CARGO SHIPS; FERRIES; FLATBOATS; GREAT LAKES; MOTORBOATS; RAFTS; SAILBOATS; ST. LAWRENCE SEAWAY; STEAMBOATS; TANKERS; TUGBOATS.

Roads

In many ways, the idea of transportation—the movement of people or goods from one place to another—began with roads. Before roads, overland travel was difficult and traveling by any type of wheeled vehicle was almost impossible. Roads made trade among early people possible and contributed to the development of urban civilizations. Even today, most overland transportation still relies on roads.

History of Roads

Long before the development of roads, migrating animals created trails by trampling the ground with their feet. Early humans often followed these animal paths, and in some places people still use such trails. In the 1800s American settlers in the West traveled along prehistoric buffalo trails, and many modern roads and highways in the United States follow these same routes.

Early Pathways and Roads. With the rise of agriculture around 9000 B.C., humans began to live in settled communities, and the need for reliable pathways increased. While animal trails had been useful before, people now began to develop their own systems of paths leading to fields, sources of water, and nearby villages. In time they extended

At its height, the Roman Empire contained some 53,000 miles (85,277 km) of well-engineered roads, stretching throughout Europe, the Middle East, and North Africa.

the paths over various types of terrain to link more distant communities as well.

By around 3000 B.C., civilizations in Asia and the Middle East had begun to improve existing pathways by smoothing them down and covering them with crushed rocks, sand, and sometimes large flat stones. Early road builders included the Chinese, the Assyrians, the Babylonians, and the Persians. Roads became essential for the movement of armies and communications as well as for trade.

The most highly skilled road builders of the ancient world were the Romans. At its height, the Roman Empire contained some 53,000 miles (85,277 km) of well-engineered roads, stretching throughout much of Europe, the Middle East, and North Africa. After the fall of Rome in the late A.D. 400s, road building virtually came to a halt in Europe, and people continued to use the old Roman roads.

Rise of Modern Roads.

In the ancient world, roads were built and maintained by the state—its ruler or army. By contrast, in the many kingdoms that arose in Europe in the Middle Ages, towns and individual landowners took charge of building and repairing roads. As a result, most roads remained in poor condition. By the 1400s, however, travel and trade throughout Europe had begun to increase, and this led to greater dependence on roads.

Beginning in the 1700s, private toll roads called turnpikes became popular in Europe. They usually followed the routes of earlier roads, and many made enough money from tolls to keep them in good repair. A few states in the eastern United States built turnpikes to connect farming areas, markets, and ports, but toll roads were built by private companies.

Road construction in both the United States and Europe increased during the 1700s to provide better means of transportation and communication. The development of railroads in the early 1800s ended this era of aggressive road building, but only temporarily. Trains could travel long distances much faster than horse-drawn vehicles on roads, and they could also carry cargo more cheaply. However, the invention of the bicycle and the automobile soon led to new interest in roads.

By the 1880s many city dwellers in the United States enjoyed riding to the countryside on bicycles. However, poor roads often made these excursions difficult and uncomfortable. Bicycle organizations, such as the League of American Wheelmen, led an energetic campaign to improve roads beyond the center of cities.

Motor vehicles began to have an effect on road building in the early 1900s. Automobiles and trucks destroyed many roads designed only for horse-drawn vehicles. As the number of motor vehicles increased, so did the demand for better roads. After World War I the U.S. government became more involved in road construction, passing laws that provided funding to state and local governments for roads. This resulted in a new road building boom.

The era of modern highways began in Europe but reached its peak in the United States. Italian highways known as *autostrada,* built in the 1920s, were the first roads designed specifically for motor vehicles. Even more advanced roads were built in Germany in the 1930s. Impressed by

Road Roots

Lane, boulevard, and *highway* are among the many words for road. But the earliest terms were probably *path* and *way. Path* originally meant "earth beaten down by foot"; *way* came from the idea of movement or travel. The origin of *way* can be traced to the word *vah* in Sanskrit, an ancient language of India. *Vah* is also the root of the terms *vehicle* and *wagon. Street* comes from a Latin word, *strata,* meaning layer. It reflected the Roman method of building roads in several layers. Finally, the word *road* comes from *rood,* which meant a ride or journey in early English.

these modern highways, the United States made plans to construct the most extensive system of roads and highways in the world.

Road Construction, Maintenance, and Finance

Road construction has changed over the centuries as better materials and technologies have appeared. At the same time, however, many of the basic engineering principles of the ancient Romans are still used. Building and maintaining good roads has always been a costly process, and societies have devised various ways to finance their roads.

Construction. The earliest roads consisted of packed gravel and sand or flat stones fitted together to create a smooth surface. The ancient Romans revolutionized road building by carefully preparing road foundations, using several layers of different materials to create the roadbed, and adding long-lasting road surfaces.

Roman road builders first made a solid foundation by excavating the surface of the ground. Then they laid several layers of gravel, crushed stones or bricks, and sand—usually held together with a type of mortar, or cement. The upper layer often consisted of fine stones compressed by traffic to form a smooth, watertight surface. Heavily traveled roads had surfaces of thick, carefully fitted stone slabs. Roman roads were arched slightly in the middle to allow water to run off and had drainage systems along the sides of the roads.

After the fall of Rome, these road-building methods were forgotten for centuries. In the late 1700s French engineer Pierre Trésaguet revived the Roman method of building layers over a prepared roadbed, using large stones for the foundation and smaller stones for the top surface. This method was modified soon after by English engineer Thomas Telford. Although these techniques led to greatly improved roads, the roads did not stand up well under wheeled traffic and required constant repair.

In the early 1800s, Scottish inventor John McAdam revised the road-building methods of Trésaguet and Telford by eliminating the bottom layer of large stones and using much finer stones for the road surface. Roads produced this new way, which came to be known as macadam, were much better and cheaper than those built using other techniques. Macadam remained the basic method of road construction for about 100 years.

Modern road construction has gone back to some of the techniques pioneered by the Romans. Builders today start by scraping away soil until a hard, level foundation is created. A layer of soil is then loosened, mixed with a binding agent, and watered to make a rigid "soil cement" that is pounded down and rolled flat. This surface is arched slightly to ensure adequate drainage.

After the foundation is set, a layer of material called a "base course" is laid on top. Several inches thick, it often consists of crushed stone or gravel mixed with asphalt. Asphalt, blacktop (crushed stone or asphalt mixed with tar), or concrete is then poured on top of the base course to create a road surface, or pavement. This surface is sometimes

Ice Roads

In Alaska, Canada, and some other areas of the far north, the long, cold winters create temporary highways of ice on frozen rivers and lakes. People have traveled across frozen bodies of water for centuries. But today, truckers brave the ice with vehicles loaded with tons of cargo. Ice roads provide time-saving shortcuts in regions where roads are often in poor condition. The season for using the ice roads is short, often only from early February to April, while the ice is sufficiently thick to bear the weight of heavy trucks. Even then these routes can be dangerous because a slight warming spell can weaken the ice and make it unpredictable.

Modern paved roads are constructed by layering different materials such as cement, crushed stone, and asphalt.

Building a Road

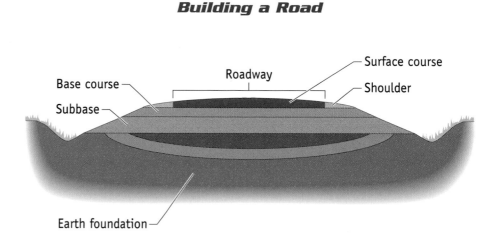

Base course

Subbase

Roadway

Surface course

Shoulder

Earth foundation

roughened by cutting grooves or dragging a rough-textured object over it, which helps prevent vehicles from slipping in wet conditions or at high speeds.

At one time all road work was done by hand, from preparing the foundation to laying the pavement. Today complex machinery can perform almost every task required in road building. For example, a machine called a "slip-form" paver can lay a concrete pavement 25 feet (8 m) wide at a rate of 6 feet (2 m) per minute.

Maintenance. Maintaining early roads was largely a matter of filling in ruts and replacing broken paving stones. This remained true for centuries. Roads built in the 1800s according to the methods of Telford or McAdam held up better than earlier ones. Yet, ruts and potholes were still a problem, and keeping roads in repair remained an ongoing challenge.

Roads built in modern times using concrete and asphalt stand up well under the stresses of heavy traffic. Their surfaces are more waterproof than those of earlier roads and less likely to break up because of poor drainage or the action of ice in winter. Still, all roads require periodic maintenance, such as filling potholes, replacing sections of pavement, and repairing drainage systems. Seasonal work in winter involves plowing, salting, and sanding pavements to clear away snow and ice; in summer it includes cutting brush along roadways to prevent vegetation from blocking motorists' view. Local, state, and federal governments generally divide the responsibility for maintaining roads.

Financing. Ancient empires built roads using state funds raised by taxation. Often, people who lived along the course of a new road would be heavily taxed to cover the costs of construction. Those served by the road also were taxed to help pay for maintenance.

During the Middle Ages in Europe, local towns, villages, and individuals—rather than a kingdom or state—paid for building and maintaining roads. As a result, most roads were in very poor condition for centuries.

Related Entries
For information on related topics, refer to the articles mentioned at the end of this entry.

In the 1700s and 1800s, many roads were still financed by local communities and individuals, sometimes through tolls such as those collected on early turnpikes. By the early 1900s, however, the growth of traffic required road construction and improvements on a scale that could no longer be supported by private means.

Beginning in 1916, the U.S. Congress passed a series of laws that provided federal funds for building and maintaining the nation's highways. State and local governments also pay for road building and upkeep. The money comes from gasoline taxes, auto registration fees, highway tolls, road-use fees for trucks, and other taxes such as those on tires or auto parts.

In the United States, the federal government currently finances about 75 percent of all highway and road work. Other nations also fund road and highway construction and maintenance through combinations of federal, state, and local funding, mostly collected from taxes and fees.

Signage and Safety

Road signs and signals designed to provide information and control traffic flow are relatively new developments. One of the earliest uses of road signage in the United States occurred in the early 1700s in Maryland, where notches cut into trees along the roadside indicated directions to places such as churches, courthouses, or ferries.

In the early 1900s, some private organizations began marking roads with names and symbols to direct motorists. In the 1920s the American Association of State Highway Officials promoted the creation of a uniform system for identifying roads and highways by number and providing other basic information.

Many signs and signals have been developed to direct the flow of traffic, warn drivers of hazards, and post traffic regulations such as speed limits. Others guide motorists to their destinations. One of the most familiar road signals is the traffic light. First used in Cleveland in 1914, electric traffic lights are now found at most major intersections.

Certain shapes and colors in traffic signs have become standard. Eight-sided red signs with white letters mean stop. Diamond-shaped yellow signs with black letters warn of hazards ahead. Newer signs sometimes use pictures or symbols instead of words to convey their meaning. Such signs have been common in Europe for a number of years. Their advantage is that they can be understood by all drivers regardless of language.

Many traffic control systems today are automated. In some places, for example, pressure-sensitive strips embedded in roads measure traffic flow at different times of day. This information is used to regulate the timing of traffic lights and smooth the flow of traffic. Many such systems are controlled by computer, but some can be operated manually from traffic control centers equipped with television cameras that monitor traffic flow.

Other types of road signage include signboards indicating destinations and their distance, various lane markings on multiple-lane highways, and movable barriers used to control traffic flow during road construction or at peak traffic times. Ramp meters—traffic lights at highway entrances that regulate the number of vehicles entering the highway—are used to control traffic flow on busy or congested expressways.

U.S. Highways

The United States possesses the most extensive network of roads in the world. By the mid-1990s the system included about 2.4 million miles (3.9 million km) of paved roads and highways. Another 1.6 million miles (2.5 million km) of roads had dirt, gravel, and other unpaved surfaces.

State and Local Roads and Highways. The nation's total road mileage has grown relatively slowly since 1900, but the number of paved roads has increased dramatically. The vast majority of highway miles today—about 80 percent—are in rural areas. Almost all of this mileage consists of state or county roads and highways and various local routes.

Most roads in the United States fall into three main categories: primary roads, secondary roads, and urban road systems. The primary road system includes state or county highways and their extensions into urban areas. Secondary roads are routes that may be important locally but are not considered major highways. Parkways, scenic multilaned

Begun in 1956, the Interstate Highway System includes more than 42,000 miles (67,578 km) of expressways connecting major cities across the country.

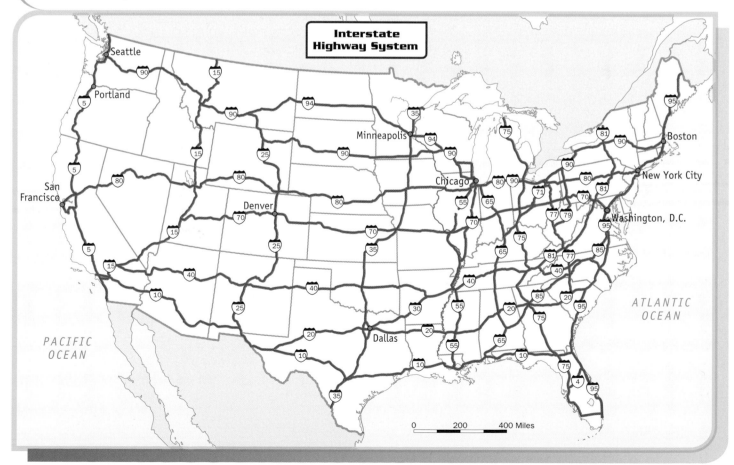

The United States possesses the most extensive network of roads in the world with more than 2.4 million miles (3.9 million km) of paved roads and highways.

roads designed exclusively for cars, may be primary or secondary roads. Highways in urban areas, the roads that feed into them, and beltways that circle major cities make up the urban road system. In addition to these main categories of roads, there are many miles of town and city streets, country roads, and other routes.

The Interstate Highway System.

The crown jewel of the U.S. road system is the Interstate Highway System, a network of superhighways connecting the nation's major centers of population and industry.

The idea for a national highway system first took shape in the late 1930s. Inspired by the German *autobahnen*, President Franklin Roosevelt and other U.S. leaders proposed the construction of a modern, high-capacity highway system that would stimulate economic development and provide high-speed routes for military transportation in time of war. It would also meet the nation's future traffic needs. Little was done to create such a highway system until the 1950s, however.

In 1956 Congress passed the Federal Aid Highway Act, which provided major funding for the construction of the Interstate Highway System. Mostly completed by the 1990s, the system includes more than 42,000 miles (67,578 km) of expressways linking all regions of the nation. The total cost of the Interstate Highway System has been estimated at more than $100 billion, making it the largest public works project in history. *See also* AUTOMOBILES, HISTORY OF; DRIVING; GOVERNMENT AND TRANSPORTATION; NATIONAL ROAD; PAN-AMERICAN HIGHWAY; REGULATION OF TRANSPORTATION; ROMAN ROADS; SIGNALING; SILK ROAD; TOLLS.

Rockets

Rockets are vehicles propelled by powerful engines that expel a stream of hot pressurized gas. By providing the power needed to overcome the Earth's gravitational pull, rockets have made space exploration possible. Scientists and engineers use them to launch research equipment and satellites for weather forecasting, communications, and global surveys. The armed forces use rockets ranging in size from small devices set off by a single soldier to huge intercontinental ballistic missiles (ICBMs).

History of Rockets.

The Chinese developed the first rockets in the 1200s. With gunpowder as fuel, Chinese warriors used these early models to fire arrows. The invention made its way to Europe, and in 1429 Joan of Arc's troops employed rockets to defend the French city of Orléans from English invaders. Early rockets were not very accurate, however, and cannons and other more reliable weapons soon replaced them.

In the early 1800s, British army officer William Congreve developed improved rockets with ranges of up to 9,000 feet (2,743 m). The British launched them against France in 1805 and, two years later, set Copenhagen on fire with a barrage of 30,000 Congreve rockets. The description of "the rockets' red glare" in the U.S. national anthem was inspired by the British attack on Fort McHenry in Baltimore during the War of 1812. However, as improved rifles appeared on the battlefield during the late 1800s, rockets all but disappeared.

Work on using rockets for space travel began in the early 1900s. Konstantin Tsiolkovsky, a Russian schoolteacher, calculated the speed needed to escape Earth's gravity and proposed using liquid fuel rockets for space flight.

American physicist Robert Goddard launched the first liquid fuel rocket—using gasoline and liquid oxygen—in 1926. The following year a group of German scientists formed a society to explore the possibility of space travel, focusing on ideas advanced by German scientist Hermann Oberth. Among Oberth's contributions was the notion of building rockets with multiple stages.

Wernher von Braun and other members of the German society began building rockets fueled with a mixture of ethyl alcohol and liquid oxygen. By 1942 they had developed the V-2 rocket, which reached an altitude of 53 miles (85 km). During World War II, Germany bombarded London with V-2 rockets launched across the English Channel. Rockets had suddenly found a new role in long-range warfare.

After World War II, German rocket experts joined research programs in the United States and the Soviet Union. In the United States, von Braun and other German engineers played a key role in developing the Redstone (1953), an improved version of the V-2 rocket; the Jupiter C (1956),

By providing the power needed to overcome the Earth's gravitational pull, rockets have made space exploration possible. They are used to launch spacecraft, satellites, and missiles. In this photo, various rockets are displayed at the Kennedy Space Center in Florida.

lunar referring to the Moon

propulsion process of driving or propelling

combustion process of burning

payload object placed in space by a launch vehicle; any type of cargo carried aboard a spacecraft

an upgraded Redstone; and the Saturn V (1967), used for the Apollo **lunar** missions.

In 1957 the Soviet Union produced the R-7, the world's first ICBM, a military rocket capable of reaching a target thousands of miles away. The same rocket launched *Sputnik 1* (1957), the first artificial satellite, and *Vostok 1* (1961), the first crewed spacecraft.

Rocket Propulsion. Rocket **propulsion** relies on a basic principle of physics—Newton's third law of motion—which states that for every action there is an equal and opposite reaction. Following this principle, air released from an inflated balloon creates an opposite reaction, propelling the balloon forward.

In rockets, fuel burned in a **combustion** chamber produces hot gases that exert tremendous pressure on the chamber walls. The gases rush out a nozzle at the rocket's back end, decreasing the pressure there. This action is followed by an opposite reaction: pressure on the rest of the combustion chamber pushes the rocket forward.

The strength of the forward force, called thrust, depends on how much exhaust is produced and how fast it is released. The first stage of the Saturn V rocket developed a mighty 7.5 million pounds (3.4 million kg) of thrust.

Rocket engines are similar to jet engines, with one important difference. Both types of engines use fuels that require a source of oxygen to burn. Jets obtain the necessary oxygen from the surrounding air. Because there is no oxygen available in space, rockets must carry an oxidizer, a source of oxygen, along with their fuel.

Parts of Rockets. Rockets come in a wide range of sizes and shapes, but they share a number of basic features. The casing, a long, tubular structure, forms the body of the rocket. In multistage rockets the casing is divided into sections, each with its own fuel supply, engines, and guidance systems. On top of the casing is the **payload,** such as a capsule for a crew, a satellite, or in military missiles, a warhead. Fins at the bottom end of the rocket provide stability.

The space inside the casing holds fuel, the rocket engines, and controls needed to operate the rocket. The rocket engine contains a combustion chamber, where the fuel and oxidizer are mixed and burned. Hot exhaust gases flow from the combustion chamber through a slightly narrowed passage called the throat and then out the nozzle, which is often bell-shaped.

Rockets are controlled by guidance systems operated from the ground or by onboard computers. Adjustments to the rocket's course are made by changing the angle of the combustion chamber, by moving vanes in the exhaust system to direct escaping gases, or by firing jets positioned around the rocket casing.

Solid Fuel Rockets. The simplest type of rocket runs on a solid propellant, a type of fuel that includes plastic or rubber compounds mixed with an oxidizer to make combustion possible. The propellant is molded into a long hollow rod, known as the grain. After being ignited, the propellant burns outward from its core along its entire length.

Parts of a Rocket

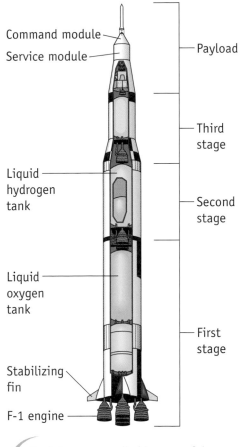

Command module

Service module

Payload

Third stage

Liquid hydrogen tank

Second stage

Liquid oxygen tank

First stage

Stabilizing fin

F-1 engine

Rockets are propelled by powerful engines that expel a stream of pressurized gas.

Solid fuel rockets are favored for military uses because they can be stored for long periods and then launched in seconds. Liquid fuel rockets, on the other hand, must be fueled just before they are launched.

Liquid Fuel Rockets. Liquid fuel rockets usually burn a mixture of fuel, such as kerosene or liquid hydrogen, and an oxidizer, often liquid oxygen or nitrogen tetroxide. The rocket casing contains tanks of fuel and oxidizer as well as pipes and pumps to inject these fluids into the combustion chamber.

The combustion chamber must be made of materials strong enough to stand up to the tremendous heat generated by the rocket engine. Before igniting, the fuel passes through tubes in the chamber walls. This process both cools the chamber and warms the fuel to prepare it to burn.

Liquid fuel rockets are more powerful than solid fuel rockets. Furthermore—unlike solid fuel rockets—they can be stopped and restarted in flight.

Other Rocket Types. Nuclear rockets use a small nuclear reactor to heat liquid hydrogen or some other fuel. The heat causes the hydrogen to expand and flow out of the engine, creating the thrust. Nuclear rockets are lighter and faster than liquid fuel rockets.

An ion rocket is one of several types that depend on electricity for their operation. A chemical element such as cesium or mercury is heated by electric coils to produce a vapor, which passes over a heated grid. The grid changes the vapor into positively charged particles called ions. A rushing stream of ions released from the rocket produces the thrust. Though not powerful enough to launch space vehicles, electric rockets may be suitable for use during long-distance missions in deep space. ***See also*** APOLLO PROGRAM; GODDARD, ROBERT; GUIDED MISSILES; OBERTH, HERMANN; SPACECRAFT, PARTS OF; SPACE EXPLORATION; SPACE TRAVEL; SPUTNIK 1; TSIOLKOVSKY, KONSTANTIN; VON BRAUN, WERNHER.

Roller Skates

see Sports and Recreation.

Rolls-Royce

supersonic *faster than the speed of sound*

The British company Rolls-Royce was founded in 1906 by pilot Charles S. Rolls and engineer Henry Royce. The two men focused on luxury automobiles with high-powered engines. Their first model, the Silver Ghost, enjoyed a reputation as the "best car in the world."

The company also made aircraft engines, beginning with the Eagle engine in 1914. In World War II the Rolls-Royce Merlin engine powered more Allied aircraft than any other. Since then Rolls-Royce engines have been used in the Harrier vertical takeoff and landing (VTOL) jet fighter and the Concorde **supersonic** airliner.

Rolls-Royce automobiles are still highly prized, but the company's aircraft engines have accounted for a larger share of its business. In 1971 Rolls-Royce split into two separate companies. One makes jet engines; the other produces motor cars, light aircraft, and locomotives. In

1995 Rolls-Royce acquired the Allison Engine Company, an American aircraft engine manufacturer. *See also* AIRCRAFT INDUSTRY; AUTOMOBILE INDUSTRY; AUTOMOBILES, TYPES OF; ENGINES.

Roman Roads

The Romans built the most extensive road system of the ancient world. At the height of the Roman Empire, the paved road network covered almost 53,000 miles (85,277 km), extending from the lands bordering the Mediterranean Sea north to Britannia (now Great Britain) and east to the Tigris and Euphrates Rivers. The Romans maintained another 200,000 miles (321,800 km) of secondary roads.

The Roman government used the road network primarily as a way of controlling and expanding its far-flung empire. Roads sped the transfer of troops and supplies and made it easier for messengers to travel between cities on official business. The highways also enabled merchants and peasants to journey to and from markets, encouraging commerce within the empire.

Well-engineered and very durable, a typical paved road was 21 feet (6 m) wide and had a foundation that was 3 to 6 feet (1 to 2 m) thick. The surface was covered with large, flat stones, and it curved downward slightly from the middle to the sides so that rainwater drained into ditches dug on both sides of the road.

Another striking feature of Roman roads was their straightness. Engineers tried to make them as straight as possible, even if it meant crossing swamps, mountains, and other obstacles. They constructed bridges to bypass rivers, and they strengthened major roads with concrete made from volcanic ash and lime.

The first and longest Roman road was the Appian Way. Begun in 312 B.C., it eventually extended from Rome to Brundisium (now Brindisi), on the southern end of the Italian peninsula. By about 200 B.C. five major roads ran from Rome to various parts of the empire.

The cost of building and maintaining Roman roads was high, and many deteriorated from neglect. Nevertheless, the roads served Europe throughout the Middle Ages, and some segments of these ancient highways survive today. *See also* NATIONAL ROAD; ROADS.

Rowboats

Rowboats are small watercraft propelled by oars. Widely used on lakes and rivers and along coastal areas, they are among the most common types of boat in the world. A special, sleek, lightweight version of the rowboat is designed for racing.

The ordinary rowboat, also called a scull, has two oars that pass through oarlocks on each side of the boat and enter the water. A rower sits facing the boat's stern, or rear, leaning back and pulling the oars through the water, one with each hand. Some sculls are built with multiple oars for two, four, or eight rowers.

In competitive rowing each crew member pulls a single long oar, known as a sweep oar, in a rowboat called a shell. Two, four, or eight rowers sit behind one another in a line, alternating the side on which they place their oars. Some rowing teams include an additional crew member called the coxswain, who steers the boat with a small rudder and often calls out a rhythm for the rowers' strokes.

Rowboats and oars have long been constructed of wood, although metal, plastic, and other materials have also been used since the 1970s. Rowboats designed for racing are often lighter and less sturdy than ordinary rowboats.

The history of rowboats dates to before 3000 B.C. The ancient Greeks and Romans built large craft called galleys, which had dozens of rowers pulling sweep oars from one or more decks. Modern competitive rowing began among sailors in England in the early 1700s and quickly spread to schools, universities, and clubs in both Britain and the United States. The sport's governing body, the National Association of Amateur Oarsmen, was founded in 1873, and rowing became an Olympic event in 1900. *See also* SHIPBUILDING; SHIPS AND BOATS, TYPES OF.

Safety

see Aircraft; Automobiles; Railroad Safety; Ships and Boats, Safety of; Space Travel.

Sailboats and Sailing Ships

For thousands of years, sailing vessels provided the only alternative to difficult, and often dangerous, overland transportation. They not only enabled people to trade and communicate—sometimes over great distances—but they also played a leading role in the discovery, conquest, and settlement of far-flung colonial empires.

Sailing ships dominated the seas for centuries. With the development of steam-powered vessels in the late 1800s, however, smokestacks began to replace billowing white sails on the high seas. Sailing ships lost importance as a means of transportation, but they did not disappear entirely. Sailing remains a popular sport and recreation.

Castles at Sea

The raised structures that appeared in the bows and sterns of sailing ships in the 1400s were called castles. Like castles on land, these structures were useful in battle because they provided a higher vantage point for shooting weapons at the enemy. The castle in the bow was called the forecastle, which usually was abbreviated to "fo'c'sle"—a term that later became associated with the forward part of a vessel used for the crew's quarters. The castles remained a part of many sailing ships until the 1800s.

Parts of Sailing Vessels

Sailing vessels range in size from small sailboats that a child can handle to large sailing ships requiring an experienced crew. Regardless of their size, all sailboats and sailing ships have certain features in common. The parts of sailing vessels have special names and functions, and knowing these parts and how they work is an essential aspect of sailing.

The Hull. The body of a sailboat is called the hull. The hull provides the foundation for the other parts of the boat as well as a place for passengers and crew to stay. Some sailboats, known as catamarans, have two parallel hulls that are covered by a deck.

The shape of the hull can vary greatly. Certain vessels have deep, narrow hulls; others have broad, shallow ones. The pointed front end of the hull is called the bow; the back end is the stern. The width of the hull at its widest part is known as the beam. In the past, the hulls of sailing vessels were almost always made of wood. Some sailboats still have wooden hulls, but many boats today have hulls of fiberglass, aluminum, or other materials.

Attached at the stern of the hull and extending down into the water is the rudder, a fin-shaped device used to steer the boat. Most small sailboats are turned by moving the tiller, a long handle connected to the rudder. On large sailing ships the rudder is generally turned with a wheel.

Extending downward from the bottom of the hull is either a keel or a centerboard. The keel consists of a permanently mounted metal plate, usually V-shaped, that runs lengthwise under the hull. A centerboard, a fin-shaped wood or metal plate, can be raised or lowered into the water. The draft, the distance between the surface of the water and the boat's lowest point, determines the depth of water needed for sailing. Boats with centerboards can venture into shallow waters because the board can be drawn up when necessary to avoid its scraping against the bottom. Keels and centerboards provide stability and help keep a boat from being pushed sideways by the force of the wind.

Schooners have two or more masts and a variety of sails and lines.

Spars. The various poles that support the sails of a vessel are known collectively as spars. The main spars on a sailboat are the masts—large

Parts of a Schooner

Fore-topmast

Fisherman

Fore-topsail

Main topmast

Main topsail

Main gaff

Outer jib
(Flying jib)

Jibtop staysail

Foresail gaff

Mainsail

Foretop staysail

Forestaysail

Foremast

Foresail — Foresail boom — Hull — Mainmast — Main boom

poles mounted at right angles to the hull. On ships that have more than one mast, each has a specific name. The mainmast, the principal mast, supports the largest sails. The mizzenmast is a shorter mast toward the stern of the vessel; the foremast is a shorter one toward the bow.

Gaffs and booms, the other spars on a sailing vessel, are poles attached at right angles to the mast to hold the sail. All sailboats have at least one boom, the pole at the bottom edges of the sails. Gaffs, the tops of four-sided sails, are usually found only on large sailing ships with many sails.

Sails. The most important part of any sailing vessel is the sail, which captures the force of the wind and propels the boat through the water. There are various types and sizes of sails. Some have four sides, or edges; others are triangular. Ships with four-sided sails are known as square-rigged vessels.

The largest sail on the mainmast of a vessel is the mainsail. The mainsail is usually triangular, attached along one edge to the mast and along the bottom edge to a boom. Some very large sailing ships have a four-sided mainsail.

A triangular sail between the mainmast and the bow is called a jib. The genoa, a special type of jib, is a large triangular sail that extends behind the mast and overlaps the mainsail. Named for the Italian port of Genoa where it was first developed, this sail helps gather more air in light winds.

A special sail known as a spinnaker is sometimes used when moving with the wind blowing from behind. These large balloon-shaped sails, which often come in bright colors and designs, help a sailboat gain extra speed.

Very large sailing ships may have dozens of sails. Each has a specific name determined by which mast it is on and its position on the mast. Among the sails found on large three-masted vessels are topsails, topgallants, royals, staysails, skysails, and moonsails. More fanciful names include cloudscrapers, moonrakers, and stargazers.

In earlier times, most sails were made of a canvas-like cotton material, and *canvas* became the general term for sails. Although the term is still used, the fabric has changed. Most sails today are made of dacron, a strong but lightweight synthetic material that holds its shape well in strong winds. Spinnakers are often nylon, a light, elastic material that allows the sail to billow out like a balloon.

Rigging. Sailboats have many wires and ropes, known as lines, that secure the masts and control the sails. This is known as rigging. The two main types are standing rigging and running rigging.

Standing rigging consists of the permanent lines and wires that support the masts and help keep them upright. Shrouds are the lines running from the masts to the sides of the vessel. The lines that go from the mast to the bow and stern are stays. Shrouds and stays can be tightened or loosened by means of a turnbuckle—a device with screwlike threads at both ends.

The lines used to adjust and control the sails, booms, and gaffs are known as the running rigging. The most important of these lines are

Basic Terms

The parts of sailing vessels have special names and functions, and knowing these parts and how they work is an essential aspect of sailing.

boom pole attached at a right angle to the mast to hold the sail

hull body of a sailboat

jib triangular sail between the mainmast and the bow

lateen triangular sail attached to a spar suspended at an angle from the mast

line rope that secures the masts or controls the sails

rigging wires and lines that secure the masts and control the sails

sheet line connected to a boom, used to adjust the position of the sails once they are raised

spars poles that support the sails of a vessel; includes masts, gaffs, and booms

square-rigged vessel with four-sided sails

tiller long handle connected to the rudder

trim to control the sails with the sheets

halyards and sheets. Halyards are used to raise and lower sails or gaffs; sheets are used to adjust the position of the sails once they are raised. Controlling the sails with the sheets is known as trimming the sails.

Attached to the hull of a sailboat are deck fittings, a variety of devices used to control the rigging. These include blocks—grooved rollers or pulleys for hauling lines, and winches—mechanisms used to pull in the lines. Lines are fastened around cleats, metal or wooden pieces with projecting arms.

Types of Sailing Vessels

Throughout the centuries, sailboats and sailing ships have generally been categorized by their size, the shape of their hulls, and the arrangement of their sails and masts. A number of different types of sailboats and sailing ships are in use around the world today. Many additional types existed in the past.

Early Sailing Ships. Among the earliest known sailing vessels were flat-bottomed boats called barges used by the ancient Egyptians. The boats had two upturned ends, one mast, and a single square sail of cotton or papyrus—a paperlike material made from plant fibers.

By the time of the ancient Greeks and Romans, sail-powered trading ships roamed throughout the Mediterranean Sea. Roman cargo ships usually had one mast with a square mainsail and two triangular topsails above it. They also featured a small square sail, called an artemon, mounted on a spar that was angled upward at the bow. This angled spar was an early version of the bowsprit—a spar projecting outward from the bow of later sailing ships.

Chinese junks and Arab dhows, two unique sailing ships, appeared around the A.D. 800s. Both are still in use in certain parts of the world. The typical junk has from one to five masts, square sails, a high stern, and a hull with watertight compartments called bulkheads. The idea of bulkheads, which add strength to the hull and help keep a ship from sinking if a section of hull is broken, was eventually adopted by Western shipbuilders. The dhow is notable for its lateen sails—triangular sails attached to spars suspended at an angle from the masts.

Meanwhile the Vikings, or Norsemen, of northern Europe were also building seaworthy sailing vessels. Viking longships featured shallow hulls pointed at both ends, a single square sail, and oars for maneuvering near coasts and providing power when winds were poor. Vikings took these ships on very long voyages, reaching as far as the Mediterranean Sea and even to the northeastern shores of North America.

From Carracks to Clipper Ships. From the 1400s to 1600s common European sailing ships included carracks, caravels, and galleons. Carracks—deep, wide-hulled ships with three masts—served as the standard European design. First developed in Italy and Spain, the ships had raised platforms near the stern and bow called sterncastles and forecastles. The carracks carried square sails on the foremast and mainmast and a lateen sail on the mizzenmast.

The Marvelous Junk

Europeans learned about the Chinese junk from the writings of explorer Marco Polo, who visited China in the late 1200s. Polo marveled at these sailing ships, some with crews of 200 to 300 men and 50 to 60 well-equipped cabins. Truly remarkable vessels, the Chinese junks sailed the seas throughout Asia and even traveled as far as the east coast of Africa in search of trade. According to Chinese legend, in ancient times a junk was driven eastward by a ferocious storm and reached a mysterious land called Fu-Sang. Some Chinese claim that this was the coast of California, and that the Chinese thus reached North America long before the Europeans.

For thousands of years, sailing ships played a critical role in trade, communication, and discovery. Clipper ships, such as the one in this watercolor, were developed in the United States in the mid-1800s. Designed for speed, clipper ships dominated maritime trade until the arrival of steam-powered vessels.

privateer privately owned ship authorized by a government to attack enemy vessels; also, the individual who commands the ship

The Portuguese developed the caravel, a smaller and narrower three-masted ship that usually had a mix of square and lateen sails. Shallow hulled, caravels could sail close to coastlines. They led the way in the voyages of exploration to the uncharted coasts of the Americas in the late 1400s and early 1500s.

The Spanish are credited with developing the galleon, a large, square-rigged vessel with three masts, a narrow hull, and a high forecastle and sterncastle. These heavily armed ships served as both warships and cargo ships, carrying riches to Spain from the Americas and sailing trade routes to the Far East.

In the 1600s European shipbuilders developed brigantines. These two-masted ships had jibs and were square-rigged on the foremast. The mainsail was rigged fore-and-aft, stretched toward the bow and the stern. In the 1700s larger two-masted ships called brigs appeared. They were similar to brigantines except that they were square-rigged on both the mainmast and foremast. Brigs and brigantines served as both cargo ships and warships.

Frigates, another class of sailing warships, also developed at this time. Light and fast, frigates were used as scout ships, **privateers,** and escort ships for merchant vessels. The square-rigged vessels had three masts and narrow hulls. The most famous sail-powered warship in the U.S. Navy, the USS *Constitution,* was a frigate. By the mid-1800s, however, naval ships were being fitted with steam engines.

The last great sailing ships were the clipper ships. First developed in the United States in the mid-1800s, the clipper had three masts and a long, narrow hull with a bow that angled backward sharply. The sides of the bow curved inward to the keel, and the stern extended outward over the rudder. In their heyday, clippers were the fastest sailing ships afloat, but they marked the end of an era. Within a few decades the great sailing ships had been replaced by steam-powered vessels, and most sailboats built thereafter were designed for recreation and sport.

Modern Sailboats and Sailing Ships.
Common sailboats of modern times include catboats, sloops, cutters, ketches, yawls, and schooners. Catboats are small, single-masted boats with one sail. The mast on catboats is located close to the bow of the boat. One type of catboat, the sailing dinghy, is popular with children and adults who are learning how to sail.

Generally larger than catboats, sloops are single-masted boats that have two sails—a mainsail and a jib. The mast on a sloop is close to the middle of the boat, rather than near the bow as on a catboat. Sloops may carry other sails, such as spinnakers or genoas, but these are used only in special conditions. A cutter is similar to a sloop except that its mast is slightly closer to the stern and it uses three sails—a mainsail and two headsails. The headsails on a cutter are usually larger than the jib on a sloop.

There are many different classes of catboats and sloops, each slightly different in size, design, and rigging. Within a class—such as Sunfish,

Snipe, Star, or Lightning—all boats are exactly the same. These sailboats are very popular in one-design races, a form of competitive racing in which boats of the same class compete against each other.

Ketches, yawls, and schooners are usually larger and more expensive than catboats and sloops. Ketches and yawls possess two masts—a mainmast and a mizzenmast—and at least three sails—a mainsail, a mizzensail, and a jib. Sometimes they use additional sails as well, such as genoas and spinnakers.

Most modern schooners also have two masts, but in the 1800s and early 1900s some of these boats had as many as six. Two-masted schooners are built with a mainmast and a slightly smaller foremast. These ships generally have the most sails of any modern sailing vessel, including one or more mainsails, foresails, and jibs.

Large ketches, yawls, and schooners usually contain cabins with comfortable living quarters that include galleys (kitchens), living and dining areas, bathrooms, and bedrooms. Such accommodations make these ships suitable for long trips. Many of these sailboats are equipped with engines that can power the ships when the wind dies down or can help **maneuver** them in and out of harbors. *See also* Cargo Ships; Catamarans; Clipper Ships; Frigates; Navies; Sailing; Schooners; Ships and Boats; Spanish Armada; Yachts.

maneuver to make a series of changes in course

Index